TIME MANAGEMENT
IN 20 MINUTES A DAY

TIME MANAGEMENT

IN 20 MINUTES A DAY

Simple Strategies to Increase Productivity,
Enhance Creativity, and Make Your Time Your Own

HOLLY REISEM HANNA

ALTHEA
PRESS

For general information on our other products and services or to obtain technical support, please contact our Customer Care Department within the U.S. at (866) 744-2665,
or outside the U.S. at (510) 253-0500.

Althea Press publishes its books in a variety of electronic and print formats. Some
content that appears in print may not be available in electronic books, and vice versa.

Interior and Cover Designer: Emma Hall
Art Producer: Karen Beard
Editor: Marisa A. Hines
Production Editor: Erum Khan

ISBN: Print 978-1-64152-035-5 | eBook 978-1-64152-036-2

R1

Contents

Time is what we want most, but what we use worst.

WILLIAM PENN

Introduction

Before I became a mom, I didn't worry much about time management.

On the professional front, I had an office job with set hours, a relatively consistent workload, and goals and milestones generally set in advance for me. I showed up on time, did my job well, and at the end of the day, I went home. My schedule rarely wavered and almost never called for structural "outside-the-box" solutions. On the personal side, however, my story was a bit different. During weeknights, my usual mode of operation was to find a last-minute online recipe, swing by a grocery store, and prepare it on the fly when I got home. Meal planning for the week was far from a priority. Instead, my husband and I lived in the moment. This time of our lives consisted of joining friends for impromptu happy hours and dinners out, carefree days on the lake, and unrestricted travel. Our free time was our own, and we never really thought about how running errands on demand and accepting last-minute invites to events and gatherings was a luxury. Life was spontaneous and easygoing. But all that changed when I became a parent.

My husband and I planned on having children one year after we got married, and when the time came, we were thrilled. Finally, a little one to complete our family! The decision to leave my job and become a full-time stay-at-home mom was an easy one, as I wasn't happy working as a nurse. I figured I could use this "time off" to explore different career paths and eventually start something new. Looking back, I now know this is when I began to spread myself too thin. Caring for an infant was challenging, to say the least. Throw in sleep deprivation, a newly formed freelance business, and my old carefree ways of managing time, and I was a mess.

For the first few years, I found myself in a constant state of exhaustion, trying to juggle play dates, doctor's appointments, freelance work, and household chores. I would often wonder, *How do other people do this with such ease?* I was constantly questioning my effectiveness in every area of my life.

I remember one time when my daughter was two years old. I was at the airport headed to my friend's bachelorette party, when I realized my credit card wasn't in my wallet. In a panic, I called my husband and told him that I thought I had lost it. He immediately switched into investigative mode and started calling the establishments where I had last used it, but none of them had it. Then, as a last-minute thought, he half-jokingly asked our daughter if she knew where mommy's credit card was. Sure enough, she did. The day before, when I was trying to juggle work, entertain her, and manage the household, she had removed the credit card from my wallet and put it in her purse. While I was relieved to know that my credit card was safe at home, I felt like I was failing as a mother. It was then and there that I knew my fly-by-the-seat-of-my-pants methods had to change.

When I returned from my trip, I began devouring time management books and articles. I experimented with different calendars, planners, and online productivity tools. Slowly but surely, I tested and tried out different strategies to see what worked and what didn't. It was through this experimentation that I found systems that helped me gain clarity, streamline processes, and get more done in less time. It wasn't always smooth or successful, but it taught me that I was capable of being a dedicated mom and a successful business owner at the same time.

Today, I run a flourishing business from home, manage multiple freelancers and clients, and also handle normal day-to-day activities like cooking, cleaning, picking up my daughter from extracurricular activities, and helping her with her homework. But now, unlike when I first started out, I use simple, effective time-management tools that allow me to work less while earning more money and having more free time.

Did I mention that I also make time for weekly yoga classes, coffee dates, leisure travel, and lots of quality time with family and friends? Using the tools in this book, I believe that you can create more free time for the important things in your life, too.

If I can do it, so can you.

How to Use This Book

Picture this. The alarm goes off, but instead of wishing for 20 more minutes of sleep, you wake up feeling refreshed and ready to take on the day. You glide through your morning routine, and you even have enough time to enjoy breakfast and a few minutes of reading the news before heading off to work. When you arrive at the office, you review your schedule for the day and start knocking tasks off of your to-do list. When lunchtime rolls around, you opt for a smoothie and yoga class, which leaves you feeling relaxed, yet energetic.

Your afternoon, which is filled with back-to-back meetings, ends up being productive and poignant, and when you leave work, you feel accomplished and fulfilled. Back at home, you enjoy a glass of wine while making dinner. And after homework and chores are out of the way, you and your family sit down to play a board game. You end your day with some leisurely reading and a long, hot bubble bath.

Does this sound fictitious, kind of like a dream? Nowadays, most people rush through their days feeling exasperated, flustered, and anxious. Honestly you would think that with all of today's technological advances and modern-day conveniences like robotic vacuums and mops, email at our fingertips, and the ability to download movies, books, and music on demand, we would have more free time to do the things that we love. But now, more than ever, people feel maxed out, stressed, and in desperate need of something different.

While there are many theories on why we are so busy all of the time, one fact remains a constant and that's no matter who you are, where you live, or what you do for a living, we all have the same 24-hour time period available to us. So why is it that some individuals seem to flow through each day with joy and ease, while others are continually pulling their hair out trying to squeeze in the bare minimum?

I'm glad you asked because, in this book, you are going to find seven impactful sections for getting your life in order so that you can fill it with more of the good stuff and less stress. From managing emails and meetings to finding your focus, creating and prioritizing your goals to getting organized, you'll be able to able to navigate these areas with simple strategies and methods that are laid out step-by-step in front of you.

But, before you jump in, I want you to know that creating new habits and introducing new strategies takes time and effort. You can't just snap your fingers and instantly become more productive. You have to be willing to do a little work on the front end so that you can reap the benefits on the back end. Changing old patterns, habits, and behaviors may be uncomfortable, maybe even a little scary, but if you want to see significant changes in your life, you have to be willing to embrace the process.

This book will serve as your personal guide to creating the life you have always dreamt of. In it, you'll explore many different time-management strategies, tools, and methods that can help you achieve more free time in your day. While these approaches aren't new, they will give you a complete framework for reorganizing your day, which in turn will change your life forever.

Don't worry—if you come upon a method that doesn't suit your personality or time-management style, move on to another. There are multiple tools and approaches included in this book. But always keep in mind, the best time-management system is the one that works for you—there is no "one size fits all" when it comes to productivity.

As you are progressing through the book, you may notice that you have some areas in your life that need more attention than others. While it may be tempting to skip ahead or cherry-pick through the information, the best way to use this book is to start at the beginning and work all the way to the end. Each chapter builds upon the next, to give you a complete time management overhaul. As you are working your way through the book, I encourage you to take notes and highlight ideas and tools that you would like to implement in your life. And if you find yourself struggling in one area, go back and review what you just learned. This is your personal time-management journey, and it should be treated as such.

Ideally, after you finish reading each chapter you should set aside 20 minutes to work through the steps that are outlined in each section. You may find that you excel in some areas, and that you need a little more work in others. Don't get discouraged if it takes you a little bit more time to work through some of the processes. Time management is an investment in yourself where the initial deposits made up front pay off in dividends throughout the course of your life.

If you are ready and willing to make the necessary modifications to your daily routine and habits, I invite you to settle in and get started with this guide. I am not going to sugarcoat this: You will have some work to do. But, if you're willing to do the work, you too can have a life where you move through your day with more ease and satisfaction, accomplishing the things that are most precious to you. In fact, I would never have been able to write, let alone finish, this book if it weren't for utilizing these simple time-management hacks.

Ready to get started? Let's dive in.

One look at an email can rob you of
15 minutes of focus. One call on your
cell phone, one tweet, one instant
message can destroy your schedule,
forcing you to move meetings,
or blow off really important things,
like love, and friendship.

JACQUELINE LEO

CHAPTER 1

Attack Your Inbox

Technology is a beautiful thing—it simplifies our lives in so many ways. We can stream movies on demand, order groceries online, all while checking our email in between. But, at its worst, technology has caused us to become hyperconnected and overly distracted, which dramatically affects our productivity.

First Things First

Nowadays, most people have ditched traditional alarm clocks in favor of using smartphones to wake up each morning, which makes your smartphone the first (and last) thing you see every single day. Games, social media, world news, our bank accounts—they're all just a tap or swipe of the finger away. And of all those apps, one stands out for its widespread use and unique capability to make so many people groan internally every time they open it: email.

It's easy to wake up and casually check your email to see what's going on. Unfortunately, this causes you to start your day off on the wrong foot. Instead of focusing your energy on your most important projects and tasks, your mind becomes distracted by other peoples' wants and needs. Instead of starting the day off proactively, you've now flipped the switch to a reactive mode.

To make the most of your mental clarity, schedule a time to check your email when you're not at your peak. Your projects and tasks should take precedence when you're most focused. By making this one simple change and properly utilizing your prime time, you can save yourself countless hours each week.

But how do you break the habit of checking email first thing in the morning? If you're using your smartphone as an alarm clock, turn off all automatic push notifications so you're not tempted to sneak a peek when an alert goes off. As soon as you get out of bed, grab your phone and put it in your purse, computer bag, or somewhere where you won't be inclined to check it—as they say, out of sight, out of mind. Do the same with your computer and/or tablet. Turn off all email alerts and don't open any other apps that aren't relevant to projects you are working on.

If you're still struggling in this area, try using an alarm clock instead of your smartphone and turn off your smartphone before you go to bed. Leave your phone off while you're working; only turn it on again when you come to a natural stopping point in your project or task. If you still can't break the habit, download the Freedom app, which blocks distracting websites and apps during certain periods so you can focus on the task at hand.

To prevent unnecessary correspondence if you do keep your phone on during these no-email periods, activate your phone's "Do Not Disturb" mode (available on iPhones and most Androids), along with an autoresponder that informs others what times you answer email throughout the day. Also, having a well-crafted email signature with essential details such as your name, address, phone number, website, office hours, and social media profiles is an excellent way to prevent unnecessary emails and questions.

If you have a job that requires you to be constantly connected, request that critical communications come through another medium, like a text message or phone call. This will allow you to receive your important messages without having to dive into emails first thing every morning. If your company requires you to be accessible via email, set up email filters that will sort your messages according to priority, so only essential communications are visible on the main window.

IMPLEMENTATION: Turning off push notifications and email alerts, setting up priority email filters, crafting a descriptive email signature, and downloading the Freedom app should take a total of no more than 10 minutes.

Organize and Prioritize

Now that you're on the path to creating healthy email habits, it's time to get your inbox in order. Just like the physical files that you keep for important documents at home and work, you should have a system for organizing essential and critical email correspondence. For work emails, create individual folders based on your clients, projects, and priority status, such as "urgent," "today" (items that need to be completed immediately), "next week," and "monthly" (things that can wait). You can use this for your personal emails as well.

When you prioritize and create folders, you have a virtual filing system in place that makes it easier to locate and reply to your messages. Setting up folders also prevents your inbox from becoming your virtual to-do list, and it reduces stress by keeping emails to a minimum.

FILTERS AND TEMPLATES

Once you create an organizational system for your email inbox, take it one step further by setting up automated filters and pre-written responses to help streamline your workload and keep your system in place.

If you subscribe to newsletters, industry-related publications, or anything else that is delivered to your inbox on a regular basis, set up automatic filters to sort these emails. For instance, newsfeeds and monthly updates from professional organizations can easily be filed into different folders to be read later, keeping your inbox free for your most pressing emails.

No matter what your job is, you most likely encounter the same questions time and time again. The easiest way to deal with this is to craft a series of response templates like, "Thank you for asking about our return policy. All items can be returned within 30 days of purchase for a full refund when accompanied by the original receipt." By composing your responses up front, you save yourself the hassle of having to think up something each time and rewrite the same answers over and over again. What's great about this is that you can create a template list as the questions come in so you don't have to do any extra work. Once you have your canned responses, just copy and paste them into a Word document so that you can easily retrieve them.

Using a Word document will work fine for storing your templates, but one trick I learned from Michael Hyatt (MichaelHyatt.com/Templates) that's even more efficient is saving my canned email responses to different email signatures. When an email comes in, all I have to do is select the appropriate email signature and the text is automatically generated into the body of my email.

DEALING WITH LEFTOVERS

MAIL

I'm of the school of thought that an overstuffed inbox visually creates a great amount of stress, and therefore, I prefer to keep my inbox at zero. Here's how you can make that happen:

EVERY DAY: During your designated email time slots, determine whether or not each new email needs a response.

1. If it's informational in nature and requires no further action on your part, immediately file it away in one of your folders.

2. If it does require a response and is fairly simple to answer, reply and get it out of the way.

3. If you have emails that are more complex in nature and that you're not ready to answer, file them in an urgent folder to address later.

4. If you're worried that you'll forget about it, you can use Gmail's snooze function, which allows you to file away and delay an email until a specified later date or time.

5. If you're using a Mac or an iPhone, try downloading the Spark email app, which can snooze an email until you're ready to deal with it (as of the writing of this book, the Android version has not yet been released). You can also use SaneBox, a paid email management software that also has the snooze function and can be used with all email providers.

BEFORE YOU GO ON VACATION: If you're going to be out of town, consider turning on your autoresponder a few days early. By doing this, you can alert others of your pending absence and let them know that they should contact you immediately if they have any questions, thoughts, or concerns. This will hopefully stop extraneous emails from landing in your inbox while you're away. Your vacation autoresponder should include whether you'll be slow to respond or if you won't be answering emails at all (in which case, you should add a person to contact in your absence). Also, ask to be removed from any group emails while you are away. This will help reduce the volume of emails that you receive while you're not in the office.

WHEN YOU GET BACK: When you return from vacation, or even after you've been away from work for a few days, your inbox will most likely be flooded with new emails that need your attention. When attacking these emails, it's best to start with the most recently sent ones and work your way back in time. While this approach may seem counterintuitive, you'll avoid needless work investigating queries that may have already been answered. I also like to schedule in some extra time for answering emails on Mondays and after holidays or time off because I know these are the times when I will have the most emails in my inbox.

IMPLEMENTATION: Going through your inbox and creating folders and automatic filters should take less than 10 minutes to complete. Once you have everything in place, be sure to file emails immediately after you're done reading them—this will keep your email inbox tidy and manageable.

MAKING EMAIL EASY

To Create Organizational Folders

IN GMAIL: Click on the Settings gear in the upper right-hand corner. Scroll down and click on Settings. Then, click on the Labels tab at the top of the page. Scroll down and click on Create a New Label. From here, you'll be able to create, name, and organize your folders as needed.

IN APPLE EMAIL: Go to the top of the page and click on Mailbox. In the dropdown menu, click on New Mailbox. Name and sort your folders appropriately.

To Automatically Sort Incoming Messages

IN GMAIL: You'll need to create a new filter based on varying criteria. To do this, click on the arrow in the search bar at the top of your screen and fill in the necessary information. For this example, we'll use an industry-related newsletter that you're subscribed to. Type in the organization's email address, then click on Create Filter. Mark the checkbox next to Apply the Label and choose the appropriate folder. Now, all emails from that sender will be directly routed to a specific folder, keeping your inbox clear for your most important correspondence.

IN APPLE MAIL: At the top of your email window, click on Mail, then Preferences, then Rules. Once here, click on Add Rule and create custom rules based on email addresses, subject lines, dates, groups, priorities, and much more.

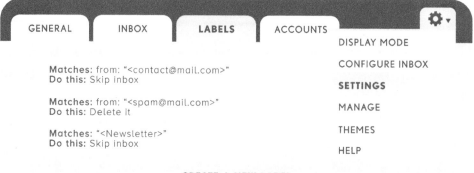

GENERAL   INBOX   **LABELS**   ACCOUNTS

DISPLAY MODE

CONFIGURE INBOX

Matches: from: "<contact@mail.com>"
Do this: Skip Inbox

SETTINGS

Matches: from: "<spam@mail.com>"
Do this: Delete it

MANAGE

THEMES

Matches: "<Newsletter>"
Do this: Skip Inbox

HELP

CREATE A NEW LABEL

Chat Asks

Another type of communication that can quickly go awry is instant messaging (IM). With platforms like Skype, Facebook Messenger, Slack, and SMS messaging, there is always someone vying for your attention. Maybe it's a friend with a really great story to share, or your spouse reaching out to plan the weekend in advance. To make the most out of these tools, you need to remember their intended use: short, concise messaging.

Before you send an IM, determine the purpose of your message or response. If it isn't something that can be addressed quickly in a couple of sentences, consider using a form of communication that allows you to go into more detail, like email, video chat, or a phone call. If you know your objective beforehand, you can prevent wasting time with a lot of unnecessary back-and-forth correspondence. Along the same lines, you need to make your point expeditiously—leave the small talk at the door and make sure your wording is clear.

One of the biggest challenges with IM is the constant alerts that can distract you from your work. To keep IM from becoming a continual interruption, turn it off or log out. Set up an automatic response such as "I am finalizing a project, but I will return your message as soon as possible." This will alert the sender that you are not available. Just like with your email, convey your IM availability to your coworkers, family, and friends so they know when they can reach you.

Best Practices for Managing Email

In addition to developing good email habits and instituting solid organizational systems, there are some general email management tips that you should utilize each day so email doesn't consume all of your time.

UNSUBSCRIBE FROM UNWANTED EMAILS

How much time do you spend deleting unwanted promotional and industry-related emails? My guess is a lot. When you are going through your email each day, take a few extra seconds and unsubscribe yourself from any unwanted correspondence. Most companies make this easy by including an unsubscribe button at the bottom; it usually takes just a couple of clicks. In addition, make sure you uncheck the subscribe box when making purchases online—by doing this, you'll prevent future promotional emails from ending up in your inbox. If you have had your email address for any length of time, you probably receive more promotional emails and spam than you know what to do with. If this is the case, try using Unroll.Me. This application will give you a complete list of every email subscription that you are signed up for, and it allows you to easily unsubscribe from any those you prefer to opt out of.

DON'T USE A JOINT EMAIL ACCOUNT

Just like your work and personal email accounts should be separate, it's a good idea to have separate accounts from your significant other. Sharing an email account creates an overcrowded space where you constantly have to read and sort through each other's messages. If they are not sorted through, this can result in emails that sit in the inbox because each party will assume it's for the other. Having a joint account also makes it difficult to keep things organized since you don't know if the other person wants to keep correspondence, delete it, or file it away. If you want to be on the same page with your partner, create a shared calendar instead; this way, you can stay on top of each other's schedules without having to sort and manage each other's email messages.

MONTHLY MAINTENANCE

While I am an incredibly organized individual, after being in business for 10 years and amassing more than 400 different email folders, I too have had to learn the importance of regular maintenance in order to keep email accounts orderly. Now I schedule 20 to 60 minutes at the end of each month to clean up and clear out any old emails, files, and folders. I download any important attachments and documents, and then transfer them to a folder on my computer. I save notable names, contacts, and dates to a spreadsheet, and then delete the folder and all of its content. While I recommend creating as many folders as you need to systematize your email accounts, scanning through roughly 400 folders (many of which I have not used in years) takes time. Do yourself a favor and schedule in at least 20 minutes each month for routine email maintenance!

SLOW DOWN FOR A MINUTE

Have you ever been in such a hurry that you find yourself skimming over an email and sending a reply, only to discover that you missed some key details? Trust me, we've all been there! It seems as though these days we are all moving at such an accelerated pace to get things done that we often miss the little details. To avoid later confusion, errors, and misunderstandings, slow down and read your emails thoroughly. Just by taking extra time to properly read, you can better understand the context, what steps are needed, and how to respond with the most concise and useful answer.

Recently, I received an email from someone who wanted to interview me for an article he was writing. Because I was in a rush, I quickly skimmed over the message and scheduled a later time to answer his questions. When I was finally able to respond, I went back and carefully read through the entire email. At the very end of his message, he noted that he was going to charge a fee for the article; as soon as I read that, I immediately responded that I wasn't interested. Had I forged ahead without reading his message in its entirety, I could have easily wasted an hour or more crafting thoughtful answers to questions that would never have been used. While it may seem counterintuitive to slow down when you have a billion emails to respond to, it will save you time in the long run because you'll be certain of what's needed the first time around.

Remember, with any good plan, it takes time to make changes into habits. Once you start taking control of your email, you will gradually notice an increase in your daily productivity.

By recording your dreams
and goals on paper, you set
in motion the process of
becoming the person you most
want to be. Put your future in
good hands—your own.

MARK VICTOR HANSEN

CHAPTER 2

Set Daily Goals

Keeping the big picture in mind, what do you need to get done today? Consider the low-level tasks that you need to complete in order to keep your life running smoothly—but also think about what you would like to accomplish in both the short term and long term, as well as both professionally and personally. By taking the time to write down your dreams and goals, and understand the steps that are needed in order to achieve them, you are much more likely to find success.

What's Your Work?

Do you ever wonder how some people squeeze so much into their days? After all, we're all given the same 24-hour time period, yet many people struggle to accomplish a fraction of what they would like to achieve. Often, important work is interrupted by menial tasks that accumulate and obstruct our paths to real goal fulfillment. One way to overcome these obstacles is to define what it is you do, as well as the steps necessary to get there, and then devote the most time possible to that pursuit.

Sounds complicated? It's not. A method called *time blocking* can get you on the right track. With time blocking, you know exactly how much time you have each day for each task on your to-do list. If a job doesn't fit into a block, you either need to let it go, delegate it, outsource it, or reprioritize.

Time	MONDAY	TUESDAY	WEDNESDAY	THURSDAY	FRIDAY	SATURDAY	SUNDAY
6 AM			Breakfast				
7 AM			Day Planning			Walk	
8 AM			Yoga				
9 AM			Work				
10 AM	Yoga				Yoga		
11 AM							
12 PM			Lunch			Grocery Shopping	
1 PM							
2 PM			Work				
3 PM							
4 PM			Email				
5 PM			Dinner Prep				
6 PM			Dinner				Meal Prep
7 PM			Clean Up				
8 PM			Family Time				
9 PM							
10 PM							
11 PM							

GETTING STARTED WITH TIME BLOCKING

One of the reasons time blocking is so effective is that all of your daily activities and the time needed to complete each one is accounted for, leaving no room for confusion. When you work off a traditional to-do list, the time element isn't figured into the equation, so it's easy to overextend yourself without a realistic view of how long it takes to complete each task.

To get started with time blocking, first write a prioritized to-do list. There are many different tools that can be used for the actual time blocking, such as Google Calendar, a traditional paper planner, or even a spreadsheet populated with dates and times (I like 30-minute blocks). Just make sure you are looking at only one day at a time, not the entire month. Then start filling in each 30-minute block with that day's errands, appointments, and must-do tasks, starting with your highest priorities.

While doing this, I make certain to overestimate how much time I think it will take to complete an assignment. I also schedule in all my everyday activities, like driving, showering, eating, making dinner, and household chores. Having a scheduled time for each task lets you know exactly how much you can realistically take on each day, making it easier to accomplish each task.

In order to make the most out of this method, it's best to plan at least one day in advance. I typically plan out my schedule the night before in 30-minute increments, adding a few time blocks together for larger projects and using single blocks for less time-intensive tasks. Beyond that, I add every appointment, event, and obligation to my planner as soon as it's scheduled, which helps to alleviate double-booking.

When it comes to time blocking, I prefer using a traditional day planner that already has each day broken down into 30-minute time blocks. The great things about this method are that you can tailor it to meet your time-management style, and you can break down the time slots into periods that make sense for your life.

USING A PLANNER: PAPER VS. DIGITAL

It doesn't matter which scheduling medium you choose—what's important is that you're using a system that makes you more efficient. If you prefer the convenience of your smartphone, consider downloading the Todoist app. With Todoist, you add your tasks to the interface and assign them to a category (e.g., home, work, vacation, family, school), and then you set the tasks' due dates and priority levels. You can even share and assign tasks to other people. Using this app allows you to effortlessly organize and prioritize jobs so you always know what you should work on next.

If paper planners are your preferred medium, check out Erin Condren's LifePlanner™, which contains monthly and hourly scheduling options, goal-setting and note-taking space, stickers, and a folder for loose papers. She also has specialized planners for students, teachers, and soon-to-be brides. So no matter what life stage you're in, there is a planner that will keep you organized and on track.

IMPLEMENTATION: For maximum effectiveness with time blocking, fill in the next day's time blocks and to-dos at the end of each workday, so you can hit the ground running in the morning. Once you figure out your preferred medium, this practice should take only 10 minutes or less each day.

Avoid Digital Distractions

Nowadays, most people are tethered to their smartphone devices. You go out in public, even with a group of friends, and everyone's eyes are glued to their phone screens. We have such severe cases of FOMO (fear of missing out) that we tend to ignore and miss the moments and opportunities that are right in front of us. From text messages and Instagram to email and push notifications for apps, there is always someone or something competing for your attention.

To find a balance between being connected and using your time constructively, you need to establish boundaries so there is a clearly defined separation between the two. When you're creating boundaries, think about your goals; this could help you determine the times and terms for when you use your device and when you don't.

TURN OFF PUSH NOTIFICATIONS

According to research done by an AskWonder associate, in the United States, the average person with a smartphone receives approximately 45.9 push notifications per day. I'm sure I don't have to tell you that being interrupted almost 50 times per day just by your smartphone is a huge productivity killer!

The easiest way to stop these annoying interruptions from stealing your precious time is to turn off your smartphone while you're working. However, if turning your phone off isn't an option, take the time to go through all of your apps and turn off all nonessential push notifications. The only notifications that I allow to come through on my smartphone are text messages and phone calls.

CREATING BOUNDARIES

One day last summer, as soon as my family and I arrived at our community pool, I realized I had left my smartphone at home. Even though there was no need for me to have it—I wasn't expecting a phone call from anyone and we weren't meeting up with friends—I felt utterly lost without it. I'll be the first to admit that I'm addicted to my phone. It's become such a part of everyday life that there are moments when I instinctively grab it and scroll for no good reason.

If you're serious about creating more time in your day, it's an absolute must to establish digital boundaries for yourself. But before you can institute rules for your usage, you need to know how much time you're spending on your device and which apps are the biggest offenders. To determine where your time is being spent, download a usage tracking app like Quality Time, Social Fever, or App Detox. Or if you have an iOS device, use this simple trick suggested by a writer at *The Next Web*: "Grab your iPhone and click on the settings icon, then click on battery. On this page, a list of your most widely used applications with their respective battery usages will appear for the last 24 hours and seven days. To view your actual screen time for each application, click on the blue clock icon on the right."

As you can see in the example on the next page, in one week I spent 2.3 hours on Instagram, 1.5 hours on email, and 1.9 hours on Facebook. I don't know about you, but spending a total of 5.7 hours a week on mindless scrolling is not a good use of my time. That's almost 23 hours a month! Just think of all that you could accomplish if only you became more disciplined with your smartphone.

Now that you know where your time is being spent, you can create boundaries to help limit your usage. While creating rules like "No tech at the dinner table" or "No scrolling past 7 p.m."

can be helpful for some, I've personally found it difficult to limit myself with these sorts of general guidelines. I tend to do better with the "out of sight" or "out of reach" method. I know that if I'm sitting on the sofa watching TV or reading and my phone is within arm's reach, I'll mindlessly grab it. This is why relocating your equipment, preferably to a separate room, can help limit your screen time.

Sometimes desperate times call for drastic measures. If the "out of reach" method isn't working for you, try deleting all the distracting, nonessential apps from your smartphone. While this method may seem extreme, some reports have suggested that removing distracting apps like Facebook and Facebook Messenger resulted in happier and more productive day-to-day lives.

If, after these steps, you're still struggling to moderate your digital usage, try downloading the Freedom app. This will allow you to block out apps, websites, and even the Internet for specified amounts of time. There is even a lock mode that prevents you from ending a blocked session, so even if self-discipline is a problem for you, this app can reinforce productive habits.

Best Practices for Goal Setting

"A goal without a plan is just a wish."
—ANTOINE DE SAINT-EXUPÉRY

Before getting started with daily goals, it is crucial to identify the ones you would like to set for the long term because without identifying what you are trying to achieve, you won't have a clue as to where to start or what to do each day. To get your big picture into focus, think about what you would like to accomplish and then break it down into smaller action steps so you can create a road map to get there. Here, I'll discuss one of the best methods for setting your goals: the SMART method.

THE SMART GOAL-PLANNING METHOD

You've probably heard the acronym SMART, but why should you use it and how does it work? SMART, which first appeared in an article by George T. Doran in the November 1981 issue of *Management Review*, stands for Specific, Measurable, Achievable, Relevant, and Time-Bound. Using this method can help you get crystal clear on what you're trying to accomplish, as well as the when, why, and how to implement it.

S	M	A	R	T
SPECIFIC	MEASURABLE	ACHIEVABLE	RELEVANT	TIME-BOUND

When using the SMART goal-setting method, you're forced to critically think through your goal and the process required to accomplish it. The best way to understand this is by using a real-life example that almost anyone can relate to: weight loss.

Start with your goal: Over the next three months, I want to lose six pounds by going to Zumba class for one hour, three times a week, so I feel confident in my swimsuit this spring when I go on vacation.

SPECIFIC: I want to lose six pounds over the next three months.

MEASURABLE: I will do Zumba classes three times a week for one hour with the intent to lose two pounds each month.

ACHIEVABLE: If I commit to going to the gym three times a week for one hour, then this goal is attainable.

RELEVANT: Zumba is a high-intensity workout where participants burn a significant number of calories, and burning calories leads to weight loss.

TIME-BOUND: I will weigh myself weekly to ensure that I'm on track to meet my goal in the three-month time frame. If I am not on target to meet my goal, I will increase my workout regimen to four or more days a week until I hit my target weight loss goal each week.

While writing down your goals and working through the SMART exercise is an excellent place to start, you need to take action to accomplish these goals. The more action steps you complete, the quicker you'll achieve your desired results. With your SMART plan in hand, start listing all of the necessary steps you will need to take to make your vision a reality. In the example above, perhaps you need to find a Zumba class that's in your price range and is close by. Maybe you don't have a scale at home, so you need to purchase one. Add all these steps to your time blocks. By breaking your goals down, you will know exactly how to execute your plan, why it will work, and how long it will realistically take to get there.

DON'T WAIT FOR THE NEW YEAR

While the New Year is a great time to set goals and make resolutions, don't allow this one date to dictate when you start something new. Each day offers you a fresh start—make the most of it! In fact, in his book, *The 12 Week Year: Get More Done in 12 Weeks than Others Do in 12 Months*, author Brian P. Moran suggests ditching your annual goals and setting quarterly ones instead. He writes, "In 12 weeks, there just isn't enough time to get complacent, and urgency increases and intensifies. The 12-week year creates focus and clarity on what matters most and a sense of urgency to do it now. In the end more of the important stuff gets done and the impact on results is profound."

After two years of using Brian's method for goal setting, I have accomplished so much more than I ever could have imagined. When you structure your goals quarterly, it's much easier to see the process through; when you have an entire year to achieve a goal, you end up wasting a lot of time because you put off tasks until the last minute. You are also protected from having a "bad year" because if a quarter's plans go awry, you still have three more periods to accomplish big things. If you're still using annual goal-setting tactics in your life, I highly suggest giving Brian's method a try.

IMPLEMENTATION: As you create your goals, also take time to break them down using the SMART goal-setting method. Next, create a list of the action steps that you will need to take to make each goal—and each step of each goal—a reality. This process only needs to be done at the beginning of your goal-setting session and should take no longer than 10 minutes to work through.

In order to say yes to
your priorities, you have
to be willing to say no to
something else.

CHAPTER 3

Parse out Priorities

It is easy to become overwhelmed by your to-do list. After all, you're trying to juggle personal, professional, familial, and community obligations all at the same time. With this ongoing balancing act, how do you know what should be done first, especially when everything seems important? Knowing how to prioritize your tasks will make it easier for you to be more productive and get more done.

Determine What's Important

How do you determine what takes priority in life? When two or more competing problems arise, how do you know which one to tackle first? Here is a simple five-step plan for organizing your to-dos and figuring out the order in which you should tackle them:

1. **Get it all on paper.** The first step in any overwhelming scenario is to empty your brain as best as you can of emotion, then write down all your tasks, appointments, meetings, and obligations in your planner or a notebook. Storing all of these tasks in your head is the surest way to forget something, especially when the pressure is on.

2. **Determine what is urgent and what can wait.** Divide your list into two columns: tasks that need to be done today and those that can be completed tomorrow or another day. When determining what to address first, ask yourself, "Which items already have all the pieces in place so I can immediately move forward?" For example, if you have a client emergency that could be solved with a phone call and a tracking number that you already have, why wait until later in the day to make that call? On the other hand, if you have an unhappy boss who needs reassurance but is busy in meetings all day, why attempt further aggravation by starting a conversation that can't be finished?

3. **Add tasks related to your short-term and long-term goals.** Once you have identified the urgent tasks on your list, it is time to prioritize the steps necessary to complete your personal goals. Since you have already used the SMART method for goal planning (see page 20), these steps should be readily available for you to pop onto your task list.

4. **Assign deadlines.** Note any pressing deadlines for your urgent tasks, then review each item in the "can be done later" column and give it a realistic completion date.

5. **Create a time-blocked schedule.** First, add your most urgent tasks to time blocks in your planner or calendar. Next, add in the tasks that hold the most *value*. For instance, if you have an upcoming meeting with an important new client and it would be beneficial to review that client's profile in advance, schedule in time to do so to ensure that you arrive prepared. In creating your schedule, there will be some items that are nonnegotiable, others that are more flexible, and some that can be dropped altogether. It is up to you to decide what matters the most. Taking the time to reflect upon priorities

before you create your schedule will help you accomplish what's most important in your life.

If there are any day-to-day items on your list that you find particularly annoying or are not sure how to schedule—like laundry, meal prep, grocery shopping, and cleaning—think about their significance. Are these tasks absolutely necessary, and can any of them be eliminated or transferred to someone else's to-do list? Is there a better way to address these chores? For any lingering items that you can't cross off your list, consider trying one of the following three simple time-management strategies.

SIMPLIFY

There are so many ways you can simplify your life, from decluttering your closet so it's easier for you to find and choose an outfit each day, to making uncomplicated recipes for dinner. For example, you might like to make home-cooked meals for your family, but between taking your kids to sports practice, helping with their homework, and running errands, there's little to no time for menu planning, shopping, and cooking. A great way to simplify mealtimes during the week is to use a meal subscription service like Freshly or Snap Kitchen. These services do the shopping, cooking, and delivery, allowing you to feed your family tasty and nutritious meals without overwhelming your schedule. I personally like to keep convenience items on hand like frozen meatballs, pasta, and prepped salad mixes for those days when I'm busy but still want to make a healthy meal.

What you decide to simplify will depend on what's important to you and what tasks you personally enjoy (or don't enjoy) completing. I'm not a very crafty person, so it's an easy choice for me to simplify creative tasks by purchasing store-bought treats, costumes, and decorations instead of making them myself.

A few other ways to simplify tasks include:

Reducing decision fatigue by creating daily routines and planning meals, outfits, activities, etc. ahead of time (such as the night before). When all you need to do is follow a preset plan, day-to-day tasks are much less stressful and can often be done in less time.

Consolidating accounts and/or information. With services like Mint, which allows you to view all your financial information at the same time, and Hootsuite and Buffer, which allow you to read and post to all of your social media feeds in one interface, tasks like budgeting and personal correspondence can be done in a fraction of the time.

Unsubscribing from unwanted emails and magazines. You don't have to clean up clutter that never arrives to begin with!

Outsourcing unwanted tasks. (More on this on pages 99 to 100.)

Decluttering your home by getting rid of excess stuff that just takes up space. By eliminating meaningless objects and adopting a minimalist approach to decorating, you will have less to straighten up at the end of the day or whenever you're expecting guests.

Cleaning as you go. Though it may seem like extra work in the moment, opening and properly dealing with each piece of mail every day—and resisting the urge to set the stack aside for tomorrow—will save you time on cleaning day. Similarly, washing dishes as you cook, rather than letting them pile up until after dinner, will make the task much less arduous; the longer they sit in the sink, the harder they will be to clean.

AUTOMATE

You probably have a laundry list of tasks that you repeatedly do. Items like grocery shopping, paying bills, picking up prescriptions, cleaning, purchasing toiletries and dog food, and so much more. With all of today's technological advances, there is no reason for you to be continually doing these activities when they can be automated and taken off your list for good.

If you have a credit card, you can automate most, if not all, of your bills by setting up auto pay online. You can even automate your credit card bill by setting up auto pay via your bank. Not only does this save time each month, but it will also save you money because you won't have to purchase stamps.

Are you an Amazon shopper? Then take advantage of their "Subscribe & Save" program. With this feature, you order items once, choose your subscription period (every one to six months), and then you're set. Not only does this program save you the hassle of manually adding orders for items that you regularly purchase (pet food and supplies, diapers, vitamins, formula, toiletries, and more), but it also gives you a 5- to 10-percent discount.

Do you have a prescription that needs to be refilled every month? If you're still going to the pharmacy or grocery store to get it refilled, call your insurance company and ask them if they offer mail-order refills. With the majority of these programs, you can obtain a 90-day supply that will be sent automatically via mail every three months until your script runs out. Not only does this save you a trip to the pharmacy, but it can also often save you money, as many of these programs offer discounts for 90-day prescriptions.

BATCH

I first learned about batching while reading Timothy Ferriss's book, *The 4-Hour Workweek: Escape 9–5, Live Anywhere, and Join the New Rich*. While this book is written for entrepreneurs, it contains a great deal of valuable time-management strategies, including the idea of batching tasks. Ferriss writes, "There is an inescapable setup time for all tasks, large or minuscule in scale. It is often the same for one as it is for a hundred. There is a psychological switching of gears that can require up to 45 minutes to resume a major task that has been interrupted. More than a quarter of each 9–5 period (28%) is consumed by such interruptions."

The thought behind batching is that instead of spreading your tasks out and losing precious time through the initial setup and repeated interruption cycle, you dedicate a period of time once a week or once a month to tackle a related batch of functions. For instance, you can batch tasks like laundry, email, running errands, ordering groceries and supplies online, chores, learning activities, and paying bills. In my own life, I batch my errands and appointments on Fridays of each week. By only running errands once a week, I decrease the number of hours I'm out on the road driving.

IMPLEMENTATION: At the end of each day, take a look at your planner and transfer over anything you did not accomplish to the next day's task list. You will also want to add any new tasks or commitments and then prioritize them into the next day's schedule. Creating your task list and transferring it to your planner should take less than 10 minutes each day.

Delegate

Even with the best plan in place, there are still going to be times when unfinished tasks and chores litter your list of daily responsibilities. That's when it's time to delegate. I know you're probably thinking, *If I could afford to hire a house cleaner or a nanny, I would have done that a long time ago.* While hiring outside help is a viable way to outsource unwanted tasks from your to-do list, it's not the only way to delegate.

If you're working with a limited budget, start with the other people who are living under the same roof as you—your significant other, child, family member, roommate, etc.—and consider how the household chores and duties are divvied up. Perhaps you've fallen into a routine where there's an unequal distribution of labor; you don't have to do it all.

Start by asking for assistance and come up with a schedule where everyone is contributing a fair amount. Call a family meeting where you can all brainstorm ways to support your household. Even young children can help with chores. In fact, according to an article on WebMD, children as young as two and three are capable of making their beds and picking up toys.

Once the household tasks have been more evenly parsed out, examine the ones that are left. Is there a way to barter, swap, or budget to outsource them? For example, there will always be some tasks that fall outside of your expertise, and while it's possible to take the time to figure them out, it's not always efficient. In that case, it might be best to hire someone who is well-versed in the task and find a way to fit that service into your budget.

TIME IS A LIMITED COMMODITY

"The days are long, but the years are short."
—GRETCHEN RUBIN

Before I became a parent, time seemed to progress at a regular rhythm without much urgency. Now, however, it feels like someone has pressed the fast-forward button and life is speeding by right in front of my eyes. Whether it's a result of getting older, having children, or the digital age that we live in, there is one thing that I know for sure: Time is a limited commodity. That's why it is so important to make the most out of every moment.

While you can't add more time to your day, you can find ways to maximize the time that's available to you. One way to do this is to outsource tasks so that you have more time for important activities and people. Duties like house cleaning, laundry, grocery shopping, and yardwork can easily and affordably be outsourced with a few taps of your phone. This past year, I started using Instacart, which provides full-service grocery delivery. While it's more expensive to go this route, it easily frees up two hours of my time and eliminates the burden of having to go to the grocery store myself. If you're interested in outsourcing some of your chores, I have listed some suggested resources on pages 99 to 100.

IMPLEMENTATION: With any overflow tasks, determine whether they can be delegated, outsourced, automated, streamlined, or deleted from your to-do list. Once you decide how they'll be completed, take the necessary steps to make them happen. When you do this daily, it shouldn't take you more than five minutes to complete.

PREVENT PROCRASTINATION

Maybe you tend to get distracted when you're overwhelmed or when you have a challenging project looming overhead. To prevent procrastination from seeping in, it's imperative to get organized, set deadlines, and eliminate outside distractions. If you've tried the preceding strategies and are still struggling to find the motivation to get started, try listening to Brain.fm. Their music (which is backed by scientific research) helps stimulate the brain and influence cognitive states such as focus, helping you get into the work zone.

Delay

Despite the best of intentions, not all tasks are able to make it onto a prioritized list, and that's okay. These nonurgent projects can be added to your long-term list of goals and completed when there is more free time in your schedule. In many cases, delaying a non-time-sensitive task is actually the most efficient thing to do, as it frees up more time in your schedule for more pressing issues.

LONG-TERM LIST

Keeping a long-term list can help you track your goals over time. While in many ways it appears similar to a typical to-do list, this one is much more fluid. For example, some tasks that weren't important yesterday, like cleaning the guest bedroom, suddenly become important today because of new circumstances and events—e.g., you have guests coming to town this weekend. Meanwhile, other tasks that once seemed worthwhile may become irrelevant over time and can be removed from your list altogether.

Even on this list, though, prioritization is key. Make sure you order your long-term items according to importance, assign deadlines when applicable, and check the list weekly to make sure nothing is forgotten.

IMPLEMENTATION: Take the time to review your long-term list of goals each week. When an item becomes urgent or more important, remember to break down the steps to achieve it and then add it to your time-blocked schedule. Reviewing your long-term list should take no more than 10 minutes each week.

Perfect Prioritization

While setting priorities is a crucial part of managing your time, let's be honest—there is only so much that you can fit into each day. If you find that you always have too much on your plate, you may need to adopt a new mind-set.

Before I had my daughter, I was the perfect mom. I'd read all the newborn and parenting books, my husband and I attended HypnoBirthing classes, and I was ready for my new role with my name-brand diaper bag and high-end maternity denim. However, like most parents find out, the baby in my head and the baby in real life were two entirely different things. My car, which I swore would always be clean, was now littered with snack crumbs and sticky spots from leaky sippy cups. My house, which used to be spotless, was now cluttered with toys and baby equipment with floors that hadn't been mopped in weeks. And dinner went from gourmet recipes of fish and veggies to whatever I could manage to whip together—often a bowl of cereal, a frozen pizza, or a simple plate of cheese and crackers.

I figured out that if I was going to survive this transition and actually enjoy my new role as a mom, I had to adopt a new mind-set: "Okay is good enough." Had I continued to let my perfectionist side rule, I would have run myself ragged. Even now that my daughter is in middle school and much more independent, I still live by this mind-set. In six short years, my daughter will graduate from high school and then head off to college, so why would I prioritize housecleaning or baking made-from-scratch recipes over spending quality time together—especially when those chores don't bring me joy?

For those of you who employ an all-or-nothing approach to life, try shifting your perspective. Instead of taking on another task and pushing yourself to exhaustion because of an idealistic picture in your head, reflect on how you feel. Picture yourself in the future, looking back at your life. Are you creating the types of memories that you envision in your dreams? If not, something needs to change. You only get one chance with time; once it's used up, it's gone forever. No matter how hard you work, you can never get it back. So, if volunteering for the bake sale isn't your idea of a good time, or if it makes you feel stressed out and resentful—don't do it. There is nothing wrong with politely declining or offering a compromise of bringing in store-bought treats. At the end of the day, people are not going to remember you for your homemade baked goods, your perfectly coiffed hair, or your meticulously manicured yard. Instead, they will remember the special moments that you spent together and how you made them feel.

When it comes to perfection, the bottom line is this: Stop putting unnecessary pressure on yourself to achieve some unattainable standard. Give yourself and others grace and consider how *you* feel and what you want to be remembered for—then learn to let the rest go. You are the only one who gets to decide what is a priority in your life and what is not. Do not let an unrealistic mind-set or someone else's definition of success dictate your task list or your sense of well-being!

I have yet to see a house
that lacked sufficient
storage. The real problem
is that we have far more
than we need or want.

MARIE KONDO

CHAPTER 4

Organize and Order

When you're trying to balance family with work and household chores, it's all too easy to let clutter pile up. But leaving things disorderly only adds tasks to your agenda in the long run, and, more often than not, those piles become sources of distraction. When your surroundings are tidy and clean, you spend less time searching for things and there are much fewer visual distractions. Neatness—at home and at work—not only brings ease into your life, but it also allows you more time to focus on your family and friends.

Decluttering 101

The first step to achieving better organization in your life is decluttering your home, office, and automobiles. Here are some simple tips and techniques for bringing order to your day-to-day life.

YOUR CLOSET

There are many different methods of straightening your clothes, but unless you find organizing as therapeutic as I do, you should choose one that doesn't take up too much time and can fit easily into your schedule.

One straightforward approach for tackling your closet is *Extreme Clutter* star Peter Walsh's reverse-clothes-hanger trick. First, turn your clothes hangers in the opposite direction so they are facing outward. Then, for the next six months, whenever you wear an item, turn the hanger around so the hook is facing inward. You can also use this method with your shoes, handbags, and accessories by turning them in the opposite direction or by putting them in a box and pulling each item out when you need it. Any items that are left in the box are items that weren't used and that should be gotten rid of to help declutter your closet. At the end of the six-month period, consider getting rid of any clothing that you did not wear (of course, you'll want to consider seasons and functions). By getting rid of the unworn clothes and shoes, you'll free up space, making it easier (and faster) to get dressed in the morning.

YOUR HOME

When it comes to attacking the rest of your home, try using the four-box method. Grab four boxes, bins, or bags and label them "Donate," "Relocate," "Sell," and "Trash." Begin with your most cluttered area and put displaced items in their designated boxes. Next, toss away the debris, list and sell things that are of value, donate other items, and put away the rest. This method can be used for any room in your house, and because it allows you to tackle one area at a time, it is less overwhelming.

EXPIRED PRODUCTS

Chances are you have expired, outdated, and half-used products overcrowding precious storage space throughout your house, making it difficult to find the items you really need. To free up space, start looking in your bathroom medicine cabinets, under sinks, and in your kitchen pantry and refrigerator. Remove and toss out any old bottles of lotion, hotel shampoos and conditioners, and cleaners; broken makeup palettes; and expired condiments, medications, and spices. Consolidate half-empty lotions, shampoos, etc. Put a reminder in your calendar to revisit all the storage areas in your home once a month to clear out expired products, particularly in bathrooms and kitchens. This will not only free up space on your shelves and in your cabinets, but it will also divert unwelcome surprises such as spoiled sauce or problems caused by outdated medications. As someone who has accidentally thrown a jar of moldy salsa into a crockpot recipe, I have learned this lesson the hard way. Talk about a waste of time, energy, and money!

YOUR WORKSPACE

Organization doesn't stop in your home; it's also essential for your workspace to be clutter-free, as this will boost your efficiency and productivity. One of the easiest ways to organize your office is by taking everything out of your drawers and consolidating, like putting all your writing tools together, your business cards, files, papers, decor, and so on. Often, when you sort in this manner, you'll find that you have a staggering number of items in one category, such as pens or paperclips. In this case, test your writing utensils to see which ones are in working order, toss the ones that are dried up, and donate the rest.

If paper and business cards are your primary sources of untidiness, consider moving to a virtual scanning and filing system. The Evernote Scannable app for iPhones can scan documents, receipts, photos, and business cards. If you're an Android user, the Adobe Scan app has many of the same features to help you get rid of your paper trail.

IMPLEMENTATION: Decluttering can be an overwhelming process—that's why it's best to schedule in 10 minutes each day to tackle the various areas of your home and workspace. Start in your closet by implementing the reverse-hanger method, then move on to the areas that need the most attention. Perhaps it's a junk drawer in your kitchen or a pile of papers that is littering your desk. By working on one area at a time, you'll see positive incremental changes without the burden of sacrificing hours and hours of labor.

Everything in Its Place

The whole reason clutter accumulates in the first place is that things are not properly put away and stored as they should be. As you go through your day, try not to toss things in just any old place—more often than not, they'll get stuck there, and that's when the clutter begins.

Before you put stuff away, take a moment to figure out where the item should be stored. One way to determine this is to think about the frequency with which you use an object. For instance, if you use pens all the time, it makes sense to store them in an easy-to-access place where you use them the most, like at your desk, near your phone, and in your backpack or purse. On the other hand, items that you use less frequently, such as your camera or a box of backup staples, can be stored in a drawer or on a shelf in a closet. Once you figure out logical storage locations for your items, commit to putting them back in their proper places once you're finished using them.

MANAGING YOUR VIRTUAL DATA

Your laptop, PC, and/or tablet probably serve multiple functions, and when the lines between professional and personal life are blurred, your computer often becomes a catchall that's difficult to sort through. Like the physical files in your home or office, you should create a filing system for your virtual data as well.

To get your desktop in order, create folders for the various aspects of your life. I like to use two main folders as virtual filing cabinets, labeled "Business" and "Personal." Then, inside each main folder, in alphabetical order, there are individual folders for different projects, contracts, documents, and functions. (To alphabetize your folders, open the folder, click on the view tab, and select either "Sort By" on a PC or "Clean Up By" on a Mac.) If I am in the middle of a project, I move that folder to my desktop for easy access. Once the project is complete, I move it back to the main folder or virtual filing cabinet.

Another way to keep things in order is by arranging your desktop in different zones so that you can quickly locate your documents and folders.

If filing isn't your strong suit, experiment with an automated system like DropIt for PCs and Hazel for Macs. With these applications, you can create sophisticated rules that automatically sort, organize, tag, and even delete obsolete files.

In addition to organizing the items you already have, be mindful of any new items you might obtain. Before you decide to keep something that will probably end up as a new source of clutter, think about its practicality and purpose. From my own experience, items like product samples, torn out articles, promotional calendars, random tchotchkes, and swag from conferences and events rarely, if ever, get used or kept. Often, you can prevent clutter and disorganization by refusing to accept any objects that do not hold real value.

Begin Again

"We are what we repeatedly do. Excellence, then, is not an act, but a habit."
—WILL DURANT, ON ARISTOTLE

Does this scenario sound familiar? Your alarm goes off, but instead of hopping out of bed, you decide to hit the snooze button. You think, *No problem—instead of taking a shower, I'll dry shampoo my hair and throw it into a messy-but-stylish bun.* But as you stay warm and cozy in bed, you never really go back to sleep; instead, you are consumed with thoughts of what you need to get done. When you finally do get out of bed, you find yourself frantically racing from room to room, trying to get yourself and everyone else ready for the day. The dog needs to go outside, your kids need permission slips signed, you can't find your car keys, and the next thing you know, you're late and in a foul mood.

One of the easiest ways to stop the morning madness is by creating and implementing a simple nighttime routine that will set your day up for success. To start cultivating a healthy nighttime routine that becomes a habit, I suggest addressing these three areas: planning, prepping, and returning.

NIGHTLY PLANNING

While you're probably not in the mood to think about tomorrow's tasks, errands, appointments, and chores at the end of a long day, you will thank yourself in the morning when you're able to hit the ground running. Quickly grab a piece of paper (or log in to your favorite smartphone app) and take a few minutes to empty your mind of what needs to be done. Once you have your list, start to fill in your time blocks with the next day's most pressing tasks. I can tell you from experience that taking a few minutes to plan before bed can save you hours of wasted time the next day. Whenever I forget to jot down my to-dos the night before (or skip this process because I just don't feel like it), my productivity majorly suffers the next day. Not only am I slow to get started, but I also usually bounce around from task to task, frequently getting distracted because new responsibilities keep popping into my head.

NIGHTLY PREPPING

Like most people, you probably have a regular morning routine. You wake up, shower, eat breakfast, pack your bag, feed the pets . . . but rarely do mornings go off without a hitch. The cat threw up all over the carpet sometime during the night, your daughter can't find her favorite jeans, the shirt you want to wear is missing a button, or, my favorite, you go to start your car and the battery is dead. The ways in which your morning routine can be disrupted are endless and, often, unnecessarily painful.

When you set aside roughly 20 minutes each night to prep for the next day, you make your morning routine a little less stressful. By checking the weather, for example, you could decide what you're going to wear the next day. Don't just envision it in your mind; physically pull out the items and set them aside. By viewing and handling your clothing, you can get ahead of any surprises like missing buttons, stains, wrinkles, runs in stockings, or missing socks, giving yourself the time and option to fix, find, or choose an alternative. Other tasks that can disrupt morning routines but can be knocked out the night before include: ironing clothes, making lunches, prepping for breakfast, programming the coffee maker, signing forms, bringing the trash out, starting the dishwasher (bonus points for unloading it, too), and packing your bag.

Of course, there will be some events that are entirely out of your control, and honestly, sometimes you just have to roll with the punches, but if you take a few minutes at night to prep for your day, you will at least have a little more wiggle room to accommodate for unexpected obstacles.

NIGHTLY RETURN

Your day is loaded with work, meetings, and long commutes— when you get home, the last thing you want to do are menial chores. Nonetheless, when you throw your keys in a different place each evening and empty your pockets onto the kitchen table, you're just creating more work, stress, and distraction for the next morning. When you are mindful of where you place your things to begin with, and you take the time to scan high-traffic areas like your kitchen and living room and return displaced items, you can start each morning with a clean slate.

IMPLEMENTATION: As part of your nighttime routine, schedule in an extra 10 to 20 minutes to look over the next day's schedule, choose your outfit, and (if there's time) put away stray items that are out of place. By tacking on a few extra minutes to your regular evening routine, you can help ensure a smoother and more peaceful morning, which sets the tone for your entire day.

When Home Is Work and Work Is Home

While working from home affords countless benefits, the obscure lines between work life and home life can make it difficult to be truly present during both work and leisure times. Without establishing distinct boundaries for these two areas, it's all too easy for virtual workers to become distracted and either work too much or too little. Having a predetermined schedule, a separate workspace, and a habitual workday routine can help you maintain a healthy balance.

PREDETERMINED SCHEDULE

Working from home offers a lot of flexibility, but just because you can roll out of bed and into your office doesn't mean you should start your day that way. Creating a framework for your day helps signal to your brain when it's time for work and when it's time for play.

It's also essential for you to communicate your office hours to family, neighbors, and friends so they don't take advantage of your homebound status. Most people would never dream of asking a traditional office employee for a favor during their work hours, but for some reason when you work from home, people assume it's okay to ask for a quick little favor, like letting the cable guy in, signing for a package, or checking in on their sick child. If you receive a personal call during your work hours, let it go to voicemail. If it's something critical, you can call them back; if not, get back to them during your off hours. When you respect your office hours, others will respect them too.

SEPARATE WORKSPACE

One benefit of working remotely is that you don't have the common workplace interruptions, like coworkers, meetings, and office noise; however, you do have to contend with distractions and temptations like TV, your bed, pets, family members, and household chores that are calling your name. This is why it's so helpful to have a dedicated office space where you can close the door. Not only does this allow you to filter out distractions from around the house, but it also helps your mind get into work mode.

WORKDAY ROUTINE

Ditching your blazer and ironed shirt for more relaxed attire is one of the many perks of working from home, but did you know that how you look affects both how you feel and how you perform? Instead of strolling from your bedroom to your office in your PJs and bunny slippers, act as if you are going into an actual office. Hop in the shower and get dressed in an outfit that makes you feel professional. You don't have to wear a suit or pull out the iron—a nice pair of jeans and a clean top will do. The goal is to transition from rest mode to work mode and mentally prepare yourself for the day ahead. From my experience, I am far more productive when I shower and dress for the day. When I don't, I tend to feel grungy and sluggish. If you have the ability to boost your mental alertness, professionalism, and concentration with this simple practice, why wouldn't you?

Organization Best Practices

Most of us are maxed out mentally, physically, and emotionally, and an organized life can often feel unattainable. Just know that organization isn't going to happen overnight; it is a result of creating healthy routines and habits and intentionally integrating them into our lives.

If you are feeling overwhelmed, try starting with just one area or task, and don't concern yourself with the rest. Sometimes you just need to build a little momentum and by taking one step forward, you can more easily accomplish the task at hand. Keep putting one foot in front of the other, and before you know it you'll have achieved your goal, which will give you the motivation and boost you need to move on to the next thing.

YOU DON'T HAVE TO BE PERFECT

When it comes to both my personal and professional life, I have always been lucky (or cursed) to be a natural organizer as well as a self-proclaimed neat freak. I am one of those people who finds cleaning, organizing, and decluttering oddly therapeutic. But even though these tendencies come naturally to me, there are times when I struggle to stay on top of it all.

Case in point: A few weeks ago, I went through my closet using Marie Kondo's KonMari method, picking up each piece of clothing and asking myself, "Does this spark joy?" Through the process, I was able to clear my closet of an enormous amount of clothes, shoes, accessories, and trash. While my closet looks fantastic, my guest bedroom does not; in fact, it is completely nonoperational at the moment. Stacks of clothes from my closet that are ready to be sold or donated litter the room and bed, and they will stay there until I can clear time in my schedule (or I'm forced to tidy up for surprise guests).

The point is this: Sometimes you need to embrace the philosophy that okay is good enough, that your house is mostly clean, that your menial tasks will eventually get done, and that it is perfectly fine to be mediocre. Being organized is not about being perfect or having an Instagram-worthy home or lifestyle. It is about creating systems that will help make your life easier so you can focus on what's most important. I don't know about you, but mopping the floor will never take precedence over enjoying time with my family and friends. After all, the floor will still be there waiting for me tomorrow.

No matter what role
you play in a meeting,
how you show up in that
role is critical to the
meeting's success.

CHAPTER 5

Manage Meetings

When properly executed, meetings can be a useful medium that contains the ability to motivate teams, promote collaboration, and distribute crucial information. However, more often than not, meetings end up unfocused, redundant, and a complete waste of time for all parties involved. Just think about all the television shows, movies, and memes that make fun of office culture, specifically the big, important (and comically dysfunctional) meeting. While it might make you laugh when you watch it unfold on TV, it's not so funny when you're the one in the meeting trying to get tasks accomplished.

Meetings: Crucial Considerations

Every participant involved in a meeting serves an important function. Whether you are planning the meeting or you're an attendee, it's crucial that you know what your presumed duties are so that you can be a more effective and efficient contributor. Here are some practices to make your meetings more successful.

MEETING AGENDA

A meeting is only as good as its agenda. What is the purpose of convening? What is the end goal? Without knowing the intention going in, it's impossible to stay on track and be productive. No matter which role you play in the meeting, make sure that you understand the purpose and that there is a well-structured agenda to back it up.

If you're the meeting creator, plan on developing your agenda early and distributing it to attendees ahead of time. Items to cover include: the objective, date, time, location, attendees, anything attendees should prepare in advance, action items, and the order of items to be discussed. If you're struggling to design a well-crafted agenda, you can use a template from Google Docs (Google.com/Docs), Smartsheet (Smartsheet.com), or a digital app like SoapBox.

Before sending out the agenda, take a moment to consider who needs to be present at the meeting. Does the topic involve the whole team or is it a more focused discussion that requires only a few key players? By including only necessary personnel, you'll be more likely to stay on track and keep the members focused.

As a participant, it's imperative that you understand the meeting's objective, who's involved, and your primary role in the discussion. Prepare a day or two in advance by reviewing the agenda and attendee list and writing down any questions, concerns, or ideas that you may have. If you don't receive a meeting agenda in advance, it's perfectly acceptable to request one from the organizer.

In fact, David Grady, an Information Security Manager and TED Speaker, advises, "Tell them you're very excited to support their work, ask them what the goal of the meeting is, and tell them you're interested in learning how you can help them achieve their goal."

TIME LIMITS

All meetings should have both a designated starting and stopping point. Therefore, if you are the organizer, you need to be mindful of how much you can accomplish during the allotted time period, how many individuals are involved, and how complex the topic is. For larger audiences and complex issues, limit the number of items to be discussed since these variables generally require more time to get through. You'll also need to be cognizant of attention spans; research shows that engagement in meetings starts to drop off significantly after about 30 minutes.

Of course, it goes without saying that both meeting organizers and attendees should plan on arriving at least five minutes early. If you are an attendee and you're running late, slip into the meeting as quietly as possible. There's no need to apologize or ask what's going on, as that will be distracting. After the meeting you can ask someone what you missed, or you can wait for the follow-up email and address questions then. If you are the meeting organizer, communicate in your invite that you will start promptly at the stated start time. Do not wait for late individuals; continue on your time trajectory and catch them up later in your follow-up correspondence. If you are consistent with your start time, after a few meetings, attendees will catch on that it's important they be prompt.

Conducting the Meeting

To ensure that your meeting produces the desired results, it's imperative that it runs smoothly and that members stay on topic. With your agenda as your guide, briefly state the purpose of the meeting (because there will be individuals who did not prepare ahead of time) and reiterate any ground rules, such as: turning off or muting cell phones, holding questions until a person is done speaking, or reminding members not to talk over one another.

STAYING ON TOPIC

As the organizer, you will be responsible for ensuring that the meeting agenda and objectives are closely followed. If someone veers off on a tangent, you will need to gently guide them back to the topic at hand. One strategy that visual learning expert Lisa Nelson (from SeeInColors.com) suggests for getting a conversation back on track is called the Parking Lot Method, where the facilitator acknowledges the non-agenda item and jots it down with the speaker's name to be addressed later on. This is an excellent way to reinforce the importance of staying on track while allowing individuals to voice their input. Your agenda can go forward and the off-topic items can be discussed at the end, if there is time, or addressed in follow-up correspondence.

MEETING ETIQUETTE

When meetings go astray, attendees often develop a negative perception that can create obstacles to productivity, staying on track, and maintaining a positive atmosphere. To help facilitate a constructive meeting, attendees should follow these three simple rules:

1. First and foremost, don't be a distraction to others. There's nothing worse than the loud and disruptive coworker who arrives late and is always on their phone, clicking a pen, and complaining about how nothing ever gets accomplished during said meetings.

2. Be prepared to come early, put your phone away, and actively listen and participate in the conversation.

3. Bring positive energy to the room. The energy you contribute is infectious and has a tremendous impact on others, so make a concerted effort to bring your A game into the room with you.

CONCLUDING THE MEETING

To ensure that you wrap up on schedule, announce that you're out of time five minutes before the end of the meeting. Summarize and assign appropriate tasks to members and transfer all undiscussed action items to the next week's agenda. It's also nice to praise the team for their efforts, as this goes a long way in building positive outcomes. When you get back to your desk, send out a recap of the meeting and action items to ensure that everyone knows their roles and responsibilities.

DEALING WITH CROSS-TALK

We've all experienced a scenario like this one: You're in a meeting voicing an idea when a coworker abruptly jumps in, cuts you off, and shamelessly chimes in with his or her own agenda. Not only is this upsetting for attendees, but it's also extremely unproductive.

To help cut down on cross-talk during meetings, it can be helpful for the meeting organizer to address ground rules for desired behaviors and outcomes before the session begins. If rules have not been established, consider adding one or two for a more fluid and constructive environment (such as, "Only one person speaks at a time" and "Due to time restraints, it is very important that we stay on topic").

Of course, there will be times when you as the facilitator will need to take control of the conversation and address repeat cross-talk offenders. Say something along the lines of "Matthew, I appreciate your input, but right now I would like to go back and hear what Amy was saying. When she is finished, we can come back and discuss your point." By heading off cross-talkers, you give everyone the opportunity to speak, and you reinforce the rules for engagement.

Saying No: Politely Avoiding Time Vampires

Time vampires come in many forms, but no matter how they manifest themselves in your daily life, they always seem to drain you of that most precious commodity—time. The good thing, though, is that you can always just say *no*.

I don't know about you, but I'm guilty of saying yes to people, opportunities, and favors because I want them to like me and, subconsciously, I'm concerned that if I say no, I will upset them or be viewed negatively. Just think about all the times that you've agreed to something, whether it was volunteering, doing a favor, or allowing someone to infringe on your time; there are so many scenarios where we feel uncomfortable saying no. To be more productive, and in an effort to not overextend ourselves, we need to move away from this mentality and communicate honestly but graciously with people.

If you struggle with saying no, here are a few techniques that can help make it easier.

OFFER AN ALTERNATIVE

One of the easiest ways to say no (without feeling guilty) is to offer up an alternative. For instance, if a coworker stops by your desk asking for a few minutes of your time, you can say that you're in the middle of something but you are available at lunch. This way you're respecting your time and making your tasks a priority, but you're still able to help later when it fits into your schedule.

DELAY THE DECISION

I can't even begin to tell you how many times I've reactively agreed to coffee dates, networking events, and other invites . . . and then dreaded the commitment later when I realized how much else I had going on. If taking on too much is a common problem in your life, delay the decision. This way you're not saying no flat out, but you're giving yourself time to ponder and weigh all the pros and cons of committing to the obligation. When you do get back to the person, you can give them an answer based on your actual availability, not guilt or reflex.

GRACEFULLY DECLINE

If you don't want to do something, there is nothing wrong with giving a short and polite no. For example, I was recently nominated to serve on a school board committee that would have required a fair amount of my time. While I could have squeezed it in, I knew that accepting this commitment would have stressed me out in the long run, so I replied with a simple "Thank you for considering me, but due to my work commitments, I'll have to pass at this time." Saying no isn't always easy, but with time and practice, you can get better at respecting your own time and politely declining when it's the best thing for you.

On-Screen but Not in Person

With all of today's technological advances, it's become commonplace for meetings to occur virtually, either via conference call or online via a web-conferencing app. No matter which medium is being used, there are some standard practices you should follow to ensure that these types of meetings run smoothly.

VIRTUAL PREP

While it's important to have an agenda and arrive early for any meeting, there are special considerations that need to be addressed before hosting or attending a virtual conference. The first aspect is deciding which platform you'll be using to conduct the session. If you work in a corporate environment, it's likely that your company has a subscription to a service that they'd like you to use. If so, find out what it is and become familiar with it before the meeting. Most services offer a testing mode where you can determine if all of your systems are compatible and working correctly.

When you send out the invite for the meeting, inform attendees which platform you'll be using and offer any necessary instructions on how to download the software and dial in. One of the primary reasons virtual meetings get started late is because of issues with technology, so ask the attendees to do a test run before the scheduled time. You'll want to inform members of the time and date of the call, but be sure to consider what part of the country participants live in: An 8 a.m. Eastern call would be way too early for those in the Pacific time zone, where it's just 5 a.m.!

SUCCESS DURING THE MEETING

Let's be honest, how often have you multitasked during a virtual meeting? Maybe it was surfing the Web, answering an email, or perhaps you had your phone on mute because you were talking to somebody else in the room? It is especially difficult to stay focused and resist distractions during virtual meetings because of their remote and isolated format. To ensure that your virtual meeting is productive, try following these guidelines:

Give participants responsibilities. When you're creating the agenda, assign roles to attendees so that everyone is engaged throughout the meeting. When it's one person doing all the talking, it's easy for attendees to lose interest and become distracted. Having an active role forces them to be involved in the conversation.

Tidy up your desk. To remain focused, Nancy Settle-Murphy, president of Guided Insights, recommends clearing off your desk, listening attentively, and actively taking notes. When people feel like they're being heard, they are much more likely to listen, which in the end creates a more creative, interactive, and productive environment.

Double-check lighting and sound. All meeting participants should check their lighting and sound for good quality. Nothing is worse than when you get on a video conference call and you can't see somebody's face due to poor lighting. The same goes for sound: Test out your location ahead of time and make sure there is no echo (and make sure all participants do the same). In a YouTube video titled "How to Look Good on a Webcam," famous photographer Matthew Rolston suggests using natural sunlight from a forward-facing window or a simple desk lamp centered right above the lens of your device to give your face a nice, flattering glow.

Make eye contact. One writer from the *Journal of Accountancy* suggests using a video format, as meeting participants are more engaged when they can see what's happening. This format also deters people from checking email or becoming disengaged because everyone can see what they're doing.

Establish meeting rules. At the beginning of the meeting, lay out a general code of conduct. For instance, stress the importance of allowing ample time for people to speak so that they are not cut off due to technological delays. You may also want to have individuals test their equipment ahead of time and ensure they are familiar with the platform that is being used so that the meeting can start on time.

IMPLEMENTATION: Depending on what your role is during the meeting, you will need to take 5 to 10 minutes to prepare. If you're the meeting organizer, plan to spend some time creating and distributing the agenda. For all others involved, read over the schedule and jot down any questions or thoughts that you would like to bring up during your time together. Once the meeting is over, the organizer will need to summarize the details discussed and dole out the assigned duties. Attendees will need to dedicate a few minutes to go over the meeting notes and schedule any assigned tasks. All in all, pre- and post-meeting responsibilities should take less than 20 minutes to implement.

Well-Oiled Meeting Machine

Even with the best preparation, there will be times when meetings don't go as planned. Members could become frustrated because the team is unable to reach a consensus, or maybe one person keeps going off on tangents, causing the meeting to go over its scheduled time. Whatever the conflict may be, you need to address it head-on so tensions don't further intensify.

This is where being fully engaged is so crucial. Often, there are subtle body language cues that can alert you of pending conflict. When you notice individuals suddenly rolling their eyes, sighing loudly, grimacing, crossing their arms, or shaking their heads, address it with some open-ended questions. If this doesn't defuse the tension, assign the task of finding additional research to back up their point, and then table the item for the next meeting. By tabling topics that aren't headed toward a resolution, you can validate the individual's ideas, while allowing time for everyone to cool down.

There may be times when you know that the subject of the meeting is going to be contentious. When this is the case, it can be helpful to briefly chat one-on-one with attendees beforehand to address their concerns. By doing a little legwork up front, you'll be better able to prepare for the unexpected since you'll know where people stand. This can also be an excellent opportunity for the attendees to vent and voice their opinions in a safe environment. Addressing the so-called elephant in the room can be another helpful measure to defuse tensions before they escalate. Start the meeting off by saying something like "I know some of the topics we are discussing today are polarizing, but I want to remind everyone to keep an open mind and to be respectful to one another so we can have a productive meeting."

The best way to reduce conflict and manage everyone's time wisely in any meeting is by being well prepared. Both facilitators and attendees should know the purpose of the meeting and what is expected of them. By having a detailed agenda and keeping meetings a manageable size by only inviting necessary personnel, you'll have a much better chance of staying on track and achieving your overall goals.

Energy is the essence of
life. Every day you decide
how you're going to use it by
knowing what you want and
what it takes to reach that goal,
and by maintaining focus.

OPRAH WINFREY

CHAPTER 6

Get Focused

The last—and what I'll argue is the most crucial—element of the time-management equation is focus. With a constant stream of stimuli vying for our attention, it's harder than ever to focus on what's really important in life. Even with clear goals and levels of prioritization, there are times in this digital age when it can be downright impossible to stay focused and on track. In this chapter, we'll discuss some simple strategies for working smarter so you can achieve all of your life's ambitions.

Stagger Tasks Appropriately

In chapter 1, we briefly touched on the importance of completing your highest-level or creative work first, when your brain is functioning at optimum performance. But how do you jump into mentally challenging work when there are so many distractions like reading email, texting, talking to coworkers, or grabbing a second cup of coffee? Cal Newport, the author of *Deep Work: Rules for Focused Success in a Distracted World*, suggests that in order to develop the habit of completing deep work, we need to practice being bored.

I don't know about you, but being bored can actually be quite challenging. When I'm having trouble getting started on a particularly difficult task, instead of allowing myself to experience a lull, I'll quickly pop on over to Facebook to see what's happening. I start scrolling through my feed and inevitably come across an unexpected update from a friend, which then leads me to another profile and down a rabbit hole. The next thing I know, I've wasted 30 minutes just because I wasn't able to focus on my mentally challenging work.

In a blog post titled "Have We Lost Our Tolerance for a Little Boredom?," Newport writes, "Exceptional things—be it ideas, writing, mathematics, or art—require hard work. This, in turn, requires boring stretches during which you ignore a mind pleading with you to seek novel stimuli—'Maybe there's an e-mail waiting that holds some exciting news! Go check!'"

While boredom seems contradictory to productivity, it may be the motivation you need to get started on your most pressing work items. The next time you're struggling to start a project or maintain your focus, resist the urge to surf the Web or waste time in some other way and allow yourself to feel the discomfort of boredom. When you permit your brain the time to be under-stimulated, you give it the gift of stillness and space that allows it the freedom to wander and come up with more creative and outside-the-box solutions. On the other hand, you don't want to just sit there and veg out: This boredom or non-stimulation period should be used to work on important tasks, creative projects, or as a brainstorming session.

Managing Long-Term Tasks

Think about all the little tasks you work on each day, like answering emails, running errands, and making phone calls. While these chores are essential in your day-to-day life, they don't always contribute to your long-term goals. To make progress in the long run, think back to chapter 2, where you learned the best practices for goal setting. You've determined what you'd like to achieve and broken it down using the SMART goal-setting method; now it's time to examine those goals and figure out how to accomplish them, since they can't be completed in a single session.

With your long-term tasks, it would seem logical to start at the beginning and work your way to the end. However, according to recent research, planning your goals in reverse is a more effective method for long-term goal attainment. A 2017 study published in the journal *Psychological Science* found that "Compared with forward planning, backward planning not only led to greater motivation, higher goal expectancy, and less time pressure but also resulted in better goal-relevant performance."

In backward planning, you begin with your desired result and create an action plan based on the steps needed in order to achieve your objective in a set time frame. It's a lot like reverse engineering, where you dissect the product piece by piece so you can re-create it from scratch. I find it more effective to map out my goals in reverse order because it forces me to critically examine each milestone, each action step, and the timeline involved to get there. When I start from the beginning, the scope of the project seems enormous, and I feel less sure of where to begin, what steps are required next, and how long it will take me to complete. This concept may sound too easy, but sometimes it's the smallest tweaks that have the most significant impact on our overall productivity.

WHY MULTITASKING DOESN'T WORK

Have you ever attempted to complete a project on your computer while numerous tabs were open on your web browser and countless programs were running in the background? Perhaps you noticed that your computer started to become increasingly sluggish as you activated more Internet tabs and programs. Just like a hard drive, your brain is most efficient when it's focusing all of its energy on one project at a time. When you multitask, your attention is split among multiple jobs, which makes it very difficult to complete tasks in a timely and conscientious manner.

In order to be more productive, nix the multitasking from your routine and focus on completing one task at a time. The simple methods we've discussed up to this point—prioritization, goal setting, and clearly defined planning—will help you be more present and focused on the task at hand. Still struggling with divided attention? Try working in intervals using Francesco Cirillo's Pomodoro Technique. With this technique, you choose one task to focus on and set a timer for 25 minutes. During this time, you fully commit to working only on this one task until the timer goes off. After you've completed one task, take a short break and then start another task. One of the reasons I love this method is that it feels like a challenge, and that makes me extra determined to get through those 25 minutes distraction-free. It also makes tasks feel more attainable. After all, anyone can commit to working on a project for 25 minutes.

Get What You Need

A few years ago, when my daughter was in Girl Scouts, I volunteered to be the cookie mom, which required an extensive time commitment on my part. Not only did I have to place orders, pick them up, coordinate with the other troop moms, and keep track of thousands of boxes of cookies, but I also had to manage the financial side—and let me tell you, Girl Scout cookies are big business. Along with all of these volunteer duties, I also had my regular day-to-day business, family, and personal errands to contend with.

Even though our troop was relatively small, communicating with a crowd of moms with different schedules and varying time-management personalities was often a challenge. I found myself frazzled many times during the six-week selling period because I was often waiting for individuals to get back to me, pick up their cookies, or deliver their money so I could meet the deadlines for the troop.

When you work with others on a task—whether it's a home renovation project, a work proposal, or a school fund-raiser—and you're waiting around for other people to provide feedback, direction, or approval, it can derail all of your well-intentioned scheduling. Here are a few methods that will help you get what you need to move the project forward.

COMMUNICATING VIA EMAIL

When your primary communication tool is email, you need to put some thought into your request. Writing a short, descriptive, and well-crafted subject line is one of the easiest ways to generate a response quickly. Instead of using a generic subject line like "Hello," craft your subject line using this formula:

ACTION + **SUBJECT MATTER** + **DEADLINE**

With this subject line, you communicate what action is needed, what your message is in reference to, and when the task needs to be completed. Before the email is even opened, there is a clear understanding of the content, which helps the reader to take action.

This brings me to my next point: what to include in the body of your email. Keep your communication short, sweet, and concise—you're not writing an article or book, so there is no reason to be verbose. Be direct, open with your main query, and avoid indirect statements like:

→ I was just wondering . . .

→ Please see the attached file in PDF format . . .

→ I know how busy you are, but can you . . .

These sorts of fillers muddle your message and are unnecessary. Nobody wants to weed through a lengthy email to try and decipher what it is that you need. Make it easy on the reader; I promise you will get a much faster response when they know exactly what you want.

Instead be proactive and use direct statements that tell the individual exactly what's needed, like:

- Permission slips must be signed and turned in by Friday, March 10th ...

- Here are your billable hours for the month. Please send invoice to ...

- Please read over the attached contract, sign, and return by ...

WORKING WITH DIFFERENT PERSONALITY TYPES

The first year I volunteered as cookie mom, I tried to impose my type-A time-management personality on some of the other troop moms who were more easygoing and relaxed. But I soon learned that, as much as you try, you can't change people unless they want to change. A better way to handle different personality styles is to plan up front, offer different options, and remain flexible.

For instance, I started off by using my preferred method of communication, which is email. But after a few weeks of delayed responses, or no response at all, I figured out that in order to get certain people to react, I needed to use their preferred method of communicating. Once I started communicating using each person's preferred medium (email, text, phone call, and Facebook Messenger) I was able to secure responses much quicker. By knowing each person's preferred method up front, as well as preparing and offering options like calendars, due dates, and rules in advance, you can help nudge them along.

LEARNING TO LISTEN

"Most people do not listen with the intent to understand; they listen with the intent to reply."
—STEPHEN R. COVEY

Have you ever been introduced to someone but been so busy thinking about what you're going to say in response that you can't even remember the person's name? I think most of us are guilty of this. We usually attribute it to poor memory, although in reality, it's more likely that we're distracted and not fully paying attention. Active listening is essential to help gain clarity and prevent misunderstandings, and if you are committed to listening, the person doesn't have to repeat what was just said.

To become a better listener, look the speaker directly in the eyes and truly focus on what they're saying. While it's tempting to want to speak immediately, wait until the individual is done before doing so. Ask questions and reiterate what they said for clarity. And put away your phone. Unless you're waiting for an urgent phone call, there is no good reason to have it out during a conversation—not only is it a distraction, but it's also rude.

Dodging Distractions

I'm sure you've heard of individuals who have 10 children, run successful six- and seven-figure businesses, and travel the world, all while homeschooling their kids—amazing, right?! These people have figured out how to focus on what's important while filtering out the rest, and one major way they do that is by eliminating digital distractions.

According to a 2016 study done by the marketing agency Mediakix, the average person will spend five years and four months of their lives using social media—and these numbers don't even account for the time used surfing the Web, answering email, and playing online games. Just think about all you could accomplish if you limited your digital usage on a daily basis. You could join a book club, take up a new hobby, exercise, or even start a business.

As technology makes further leaps and bounds, digital distractions will only play a more prevalent role in your daily life. To get a handle on the situation, you'll need to become more disciplined with how you use technology. In chapter 2, you learned a few simple tactics for avoiding digital distractions, such as turning off push notifications, relocating your device to a different room, and enabling "Do Not Disturb" mode, but what if these don't work? How do you avoid the temptation of picking up your phone and mindlessly scrolling?

OLD SCHOOL OR NEW SCHOOL?

There are a multitude of productivity apps and web browser extensions that can help you block out distracting websites and applications (my favorites are Flipd, StayFocused, Strict Workflow, and Freedom), but if technology is keeping you from using your time constructively, you should try going old school and swap out the digital apps for physical products.

If you need to jot down a note or grocery list, use a notebook, sticky note, or whiteboard. Need to schedule an appointment? Use a paper calendar, day planner, or date book. Instead of snapping a picture with your smartphone, break out the expensive digital camera you bought but never use and take some high-quality shots. There is a myriad of sleek and modern products that can easily replace or replicate tasks that you currently use your smartphone to do. By limiting the number of times you grab your device, you're less likely to fall down the digital distraction rabbit hole.

REWARD SYSTEM

Maybe reward systems work better for you. If so, you can combine the Pomodoro Technique (page 70) with a digital reward. Focus on a task for 25 minutes, and then allow yourself a 5-minute break to tweet, scroll, or watch funny cat videos. This will help prevent digital distractions from infiltrating your work time while still providing little doses of exposure to the platforms you enjoy.

Keeping On-Task

Toward the end of my nursing career, I worked as a clinical coordinator for a pharmaceutical research facility. The clinic was spread out over three different floors of an office building. At the time, I was co-managing one study on the third floor and assisting with another clinical trial on the first floor. Talk about multitasking—I was literally running all over the building all day long to manage the two studies with completely different patients and two different types of investigational medications. In this position, as well as in other nursing positions I've held, multitasking wasn't a choice. It was the only option.

If you work in an industry where you don't have the luxury of monotasking, such as event planning, waiting tables, nursing, or answering phones, here are a few techniques that will help keep you on track and prevent you from getting overwhelmed.

USE A CHEAT SHEET

When I worked as a nurse, I could not live without my hourly time-management sheet. At the beginning of a work shift, I'd fill in the patient's information, including room number, diagnosis, and times that medications needed to be dispensed. Having to manage multiple patients with different acuity levels who were taking a wide variety of drugs, I couldn't have possibly remembered every important piece of information without writing it down. This worksheet was my "extra brain," and I kept it in my pocket at all times so I would always be prepared.

PRIORITIZE

Many times, when I was in the middle of assessing one patient, another call light would go off, indicating someone in need of assistance. Maybe they were vomiting, running a fever, or in pain; whatever the case may have been, I was constantly reassessing my patients' needs and prioritizing (and then reprioritizing) which task would be completed next. If you work in a multitasking type of position, it's very likely that you constantly have to readjust your schedule based on what's happening at any given moment. To do this effectively, you must be able to instantly determine what's urgent (what needs to be done immediately to prevent negative consequences) versus what's important (items that need to be completed in a timely manner). At times, you may need to delegate or rearrange what gets done next—the key is that you need to be flexible so you can adapt to the changes as they occur.

CONSOLIDATE AND STREAMLINE PROCESSES

Depending on your occupation, there will be different ways in which you can streamline and consolidate tasks for maximum efficiency. Perhaps it's reducing the number of apps that you use, or maybe it's creating automated systems for repetitive tasks. No matter where you work or what you do, there are ways in which you can improve your efficiency by coming up with systems that streamline your workflow. For instance, when I worked at the hospital, I wore scrubs with extra-large cargo pockets where I could store frequently used supplies so I always had what I needed. By doing this, I eliminated unnecessary trips to the supply room or nursing station, saving me time that I didn't have in the first place.

> **IMPLEMENTATION:** Breaking down your long-term goals in reverse order and adding the appropriate steps to your calendar should take approximately 15 to 20 minutes. If you find that it's taking you more time, give yourself a break and come back to it later. I find that when I'm having a challenging time figuring something out, a short break can help my brain subconsciously work out the details on its own.

Keeping Yourself in Mind

You've probably wondered again and again, *How do some people manage to squeeze so much out of their days while I struggle to complete the bare necessities?* Maybe you've dreamed about a life where there's plenty of time for you to do all the activities you enjoy. For you and an ever-growing number of individuals, more efficient time management seems to be far out of reach.

The good news is that filling your life with more of the things you'd like to do and accomplish is more than possible with a little discipline and some minor tweaks to your daily habits.

Follow the Steps

I understand what it's like to be frazzled, disorganized, and always strapped for time. But I also know that complaining and wishing for more time in the day won't help you achieve anything—you have to be willing to make adjustments and learn new habits. The good news is that by picking up this book and reading it to this point, you've proven that you're ready to do what it takes to implement more efficient systems and make better use of your time.

You already have all the tools you need for the strategies outlined in the book, and once you start using them, you'll notice that your life will change for the better. Utilizing these methods will give you more time to focus on the things that matter most to you—whether it's taking time off for vacations, learning a new hobby, or simply spending more time with family and friends. If you find yourself struggling in one area, go back and reread your highlighted text. And be sure to also check out the Resources section in the back of this book (page 95), where I've listed many more tools that can help you find a better time-management strategy.

Give Yourself a Break

"When the well's dry, we know the worth of water."
—BENJAMIN FRANKLIN

Has this ever happened to you? You're sitting at your desk trying to figure out how you're going to accomplish everything on your to-do list. You have a big project looming overhead, tons of paperwork, and a PTO meeting to attend that evening, so you start eliminating all forms of self-care from your schedule. You skip lunch, grab another cup of coffee, cancel your Pilates class, pick up fast food through the drive-thru, and then work all night until you can no longer keep your eyes open. The next day is more of the same, but now you're feeling run-down, irritated, and exhausted. When you get home from work, you snap at your kids, burn dinner, and, finally, you go to bed feeling angry and defeated.

Self-care is not self-indulgent; it is a necessary component to maintaining your well-being and staying on track. While you may think of self-care as a luxury like going to the spa or getting a pedicure, it is so much more complex. In a *Psychology Today* article titled "Self-Care in a Toxic World," psychologist Christine Meinecke PhD defines self-care as "choosing behaviors that balance the effects of emotional and physical stressors: exercising, eating healthy foods, getting enough sleep, practicing yoga or meditation or relaxation techniques, abstaining from substance abuse, pursuing creative outlets, engaging in psychotherapy."

When you have too much on your plate, it may seem counterintuitive to stop and take a short break. But the truth is that if you keep pushing yourself when you're mentally exhausted, you will become irritable and stressed, and you'll have a difficult time focusing. Taking breaks, eating healthy foods, meditating, and physical activity all help to refuel your tank, which is precisely what you need when you're out of gas.

The good news is that you don't have to spend a massive amount of time to recharge your batteries; often, a simple 15-minute break will do. According to Tony Schwartz, CEO of the Energy Project, "Focus in the most absorbed way possible when you are working and then take a break at least every 90 minutes to refuel your energy reservoir. Any activity—like deep breathing, reading a novel, talking with a friend or taking a run—can be effective. The key is choosing something you find restorative."

Do What Works for You

In chapter 1, we talked about doing your most important work first thing in the morning when your mind is refreshed, but some people are genetically night owls, meaning that their sleep length, timing, and circadian rhythms differ from their counterparts, the early birds. According to an article published on the website New Medical Life Sciences entitled "Circadian Rhythm Length Variations," "The sleep-wake schedule differs between individuals, and is most obvious in relation to morning or evening alertness. Some people are morning type individuals (or 'larks'), and wake early, peak early, but wind down relatively early in the night. Others (the 'night owls') wake only by late morning or mid-day but have peak productivity in the evening or at night and sleep late."

If you are a night owl, tackle the least critical tasks in the morning and then focus on the most important tasks later when you're more alert. There is no "one size fits all" in time management, only suggestions and tips for strategies that have worked well for others and that may work for you. You need to experiment with different techniques to see what works best for your personality and situation.

When I first started experimenting with time-management techniques, I tried out a ton of different apps and planners. I first purchased this sleek leather pocket planner that fit perfectly in my purse; it was the size of a checkbook. But after using it for a few weeks, I realized it wasn't very practical, that there wasn't enough room to write out all of my tasks, appointments, and to-dos on the mini calendar and note space. Over the next couple of years, I tested numerous day planners and smartphone apps until I found the system that worked right for me. The key is to try different strategies and systems; often you won't know if they work until you've used them for a while.

Commit to the Process

No matter what you want to accomplish—whether it's getting a college degree, learning a musical instrument, or becoming better at time management—you have to commit to the process. There is no magic potion; none of it will work unless you put in the effort. The good news is that all of the productivity strategies in this book are straightforward and simple to implement.

When you're working toward goal attainment, there may be times when you decide the process isn't working for you and you want to give up. If this happens and you feel uninspired, you need to go back to your "why." Write down the reasons you want to achieve better time management, such as spending more time with your family, going on more vacations, or starting a business. Having clear objectives can be a powerful motivator to keep going when things become challenging.

GET BACK ON TRACK

There will be times when you fall out of your newly formed habits. When this happens, pick back up where you left off and start again. I'll admit that when the weekend rolls around, I'm ready to put work aside and enjoy my free time. Because of this, there are times when I skip my Sunday night time-blocking session for the coming week. I think to myself, *I'll be fine without my list. I'll remember what I need to do.* But then, come Monday, I'm slow to get started, not as focused, and not as productive as I usually am. The beautiful thing about time management is that each day offers you a clean slate. If you get sidetracked or fall out of your routine, you can always refocus and start again tomorrow.

REINFORCING GOOD HABITS

I choose to exercise outside of my home because I find that when there's an instructor to hold me accountable, I push myself harder. When I work out at home, I'm way more likely to go easy on myself or skip it altogether. Having an accountability partner can be a compelling way to reinforce good habits. If you find that you're having trouble committing to the process, ask a trusted friend or family member (ideally, someone else who is also struggling in this area) to be your personal motivator.

Having someone keep tabs on what you're doing will help you stay on track. If rewards motivate you, create a system where you treat yourself to a prize when you achieve your goals. I have found that a combination of the two works extremely well in reinforcing positive habits.

Take Your Time

If you find that you're becoming overwhelmed with the process, slow down. There is no deadline for completing the strategies in this book. All of the exercises can be implemented one at a time, but as you go, you'll notice that they build on each other, gradually freeing up more and more space in your day. As long as you're committed and you're setting aside a little time each day to implement the methods, you'll become better at being a master of your time. Remember, time management is a learning process; you have to figure out what systems work best for you. The goal is to keep placing one foot in front of the other until you've finally reached your destination.

THERE IS NO WRONG WAY

"Sticking to good habits can be hard work, and mistakes are part of the process. Don't declare failure simply because you messed up or because you're having trouble reaching your goals. Instead, use your mistakes as opportunities to grow stronger and become better."

—AMY MORIN

Most people tend to see things either as black or white, right or wrong; but with time management, there are no right or wrong answers. There are only strategies and methods, and some may work for you, while others may not. The only way to be sure is by testing out the various techniques and observing which ones make a significant impact on your day. For the longest time, I tried to manage all of my calendars and agendas digitally, as that seemed most intuitive. But what I found through my trial-and-error process is that I'm more inclined to keep up with physical products such as day planners and notebooks. Had I not explored all my options and tried out different methods, I would never have been able to accomplish all that I have in my business and personal life.

COMING UP WITH YOUR OWN SYSTEMS

As you train yourself to be more efficient, you may come up with your own unique systems. In my own life, I've come up with the Stop Waiting Around method. For instance, whenever I'm heating something up in the microwave, I challenge myself to see how many tasks I can complete while the timer is running down. Usually, I can load or unload the dishwasher, clean off the countertops, or sort through my mail. Instead of idly waiting around for things to happen, I use these micro-units of time to knock things out.

Each day, I apply this mind-set to the time that I have available to me. If I'm sitting at the doctor's office waiting to be called, instead of leafing through a magazine that I have no interest in, I choose to read a book, do some brainstorming, or answer some emails on my smartphone. In the morning when we're waiting for the school bus to arrive, I'll go over math concepts with my daughter. We all have small pockets of time in our days that can be optimized for greater productivity.

Be Intentional

"How we spend our days is, of course, how we spend our lives. What we do with this hour, and that one, is what we are doing. A schedule defends from chaos and whim. It is a net for catching days. It is a scaffolding on which a worker can stand and labor with both hands at sections of time. A schedule is a mock-up of reason and order—willed, faked, and so brought into being; it is a peace and a haven set into the wreck of time; it is a lifeboat on which you find yourself, decades later, still living."
—ANNIE DILLARD

When you get right down to it, time management is all about making small conscious decisions to be intentional with your actions. You can choose to scroll through Instagram for 30 minutes or you can choose to read a book that will benefit your career. You can opt to watch TV or you can use that time to go to the gym and work out—it's your choice. If you're ready to become more intentional, take a moment to write down what your ideal life looks and feels like.

WHAT'S YOUR IDEAL LIFE?

Start with your morning routine. Picture it in your head. In your perfect life: How would you like your day to begin? Do you wake up refreshed, joyful, and ready to take on the day? Do you picture yourself reading the morning paper and sipping on coffee while your family eats breakfast next to you? Do you see yourself attending yoga before you head to work? Do this exercise for your entire day, including all the little details, such as how you look, what activities you're doing, and, most important, how you feel when you're doing each activity. When you complete this exercise, it's important to note which things didn't make your list, such as spending time on social media or playing games.

Once you have your ideal scenario written down, start investigating the little ways in which you can make your ideal life a reality. There's no need to make big sweeping changes—when you try to change too much too quickly, it's usually overwhelming. For myself, when I start to feel frazzled in one area, I look for little aspects that I can modify to make my life simpler. For instance, weekday mornings are hectic in our household. Everyone's scurrying around trying to get ready quickly so they can make it out of the door on time. I used to get so overwhelmed by all the tasks I had to complete in the midst of this morning chaos that I was constantly frustrated and irritable—not the best way to start the day. To create a more peaceful morning routine, I started waking up just 15 minutes earlier, and presetting the coffee maker and making my daughter's lunch the night before. By making these simple modifications, I gave myself the luxury of spending a little more quality time with my daughter each morning before she heads out to school. It's such a wonderful way for me to ease into my day, instead of feeling stressed out before I've even begun.

CREATE A "STOP DOING THAT" LIST

You've obviously heard of the to-do list, but have you ever thought about creating a not-to-do or "stop doing that" list? I hadn't either until I read about this method on author and inspirational speaker Danielle LaPorte's blog. Over the years, I've used this strategy many times to help let go of habits and activities that are not serving me well, and it's been transformational. When you get crystal clear on what you *don't* want in your life, you become more focused on the things that you *do* want. Danielle writes, "On the path to defining your own version of success, what you stop doing is just as important as the things you start doing."

Things that I've included on my own "stop doing that" list are:

→ Overextending myself

→ Scrolling without purpose

→ Worrying about things I can't change

→ Watching recipe creation videos

→ Reading negative comments on articles

→ Mindlessly checking my smartphone

DEFINE SUCCESS ON YOUR OWN TERMS

There are times when I'm guilty of always creating bigger and better goals and, as a result, not allowing myself to feel successful. The problem with this mind-set, as happiness expert and researcher Shawn Achor writes on his blog, is that "happiness fuels success and not the other way around. The problem with putting success before happiness is that success is a moving target—once you achieve a victory (something you thought would bring happiness) you push the goal post out, so happiness keeps getting pushed over the horizon."

Years ago, I was inspired by a business coach who, through a revenue model, pushed her clients to expand and crystallize their goals. While these methods were successful in creating bigger outcomes for my business, they weren't in alignment with my core values. In fact, when I look back, I realize that I was stressed, feeling uncertain, and not doing what I wanted to do in my free time, which was spending quality time with my family and friends.

What I've learned along the way is that you are the only one who can define the terms for success in your life. When you're coming up with those parameters, be sure that you're keeping your "why" front and center. When you work on goals and define success based on things that bring you fulfillment, you'll find that your productivity soars because you're focusing on what is truly important and what feeds your soul.

Time-Blocking Chart

If you prefer a non-digital means of organization, the following template can be photocopied and used as a weekly time-blocking chart.

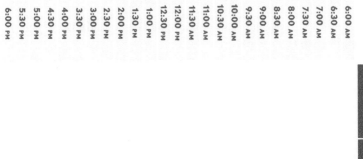

Resources

Books

168 Hours: You Have More Time Than You Think by Laura Vanderkam (Portfolio, 2011)

Eat That Frog!: 21 Great Ways to Stop Procrastinating and Get More Done in Less Time by Brian Tracy (Berrett-Koehler Publishers, 2017)

The 4-Hour Workweek: Escape 9–5, Live Anywhere, and Join the New Rich by Timothy Ferriss (Harmony, 2009)

Getting Things Done: The Art of Stress-Free Productivity by David Allen (Penguin, 2015)

The Life-Changing Magic of Tidying Up: The Japanese Art of Decluttering and Organizing by Marie Kondo (Ten Speed Press, 2014)

The Miracle Morning: The Not-So-Obvious Secret Guaranteed to Transform Your Life (Before 8AM) by Hal Elrod (Hal Elrod International, Inc., 2012)

The 12 Week Year: Get More Done in 12 Weeks than Others Do in 12 Months by Brian P. Moran (Wiley, 2013)

Your Best Year Ever: A 5-Step Plan for Achieving Your Most Important Goals by Michael Hyatt (Baker Books, 2018)

Productivity Apps

Asana
Asana.com

Cozi
Cozi.com

Evernote
Evernote.com

Flipd
FlipdApp.co

OmniFocus
OmniGroup.com/OmniFocus

Remember the Milk
RememberTheMilk.com

Rescue Time
RescueTime.com

SoapBox
SoapBoxHQ.com

StayFocused
Bit.ly/2Lo1EfE

Strict Workflow
Bit.ly/2J1Ksdn

Time Doctor
TimeDoctor.com

Todoist
Todoist.com

Toggl
Toggl.com

Digital Organization Apps

Adobe Scan
Bit.ly/2AXhiVd

DropIt (for PC)
DropItProject.com

Evernote Scanner (iOS)
Apple.co/2DMfa7h

Hazel (for Mac)
Noodlesoft.com

Social Media Tracking / Device Usage Tracking Apps

AppDetox
Play.Google.com/store/apps/details?id=de.dfki
.appdetox&hl=en_US

Social Fever
Bit.ly/2XYAo9k

Quality Time
QualityTimeApp.com

Meal Delivery Services

Blue Apron
BlueApron.com

Daily Harvest
Daily-Harvest.com

Dinnerly
Dinnerly.com

Meal Delivery Services *continued*

Emeals
Emeals.com

Factor 75
Factor75.com

Freshly
Freshly.com

Green Chef
GreenChef.com/home

Hello Fresh
HelloFresh.com

Home Chef
HomeChef.com

Hungryroot
Hungryroot.com

Marley Spoon
MarleySpoon.com

Plated
Plated.com

Snap Kitchen
SnapKitchen.com

Sun Basket
SunBasket.com

Tovala
Tovala.com

Apps and Services for Outsourcing Administrative Tasks

Fancy Hands
FancyHands.com

Fiverr
Fiverr.com

Task Bullet
TaskBullet.com

Upwork
Upwork.com

Zirtual
Zirtual.com

Apps and Services for Outsourcing General Tasks

Care.com
Care.com

Plowz & Mowz
PlowzAndMowz.com

Takl
Takl.com

TaskEasy
TaskEasy.com/apps

Task Rabbit
TaskRabbit.com

Thumbtack
Thumbtack.com

Apps and Services for Outsourcing Grocery Shopping

Amazon Fresh
Amazon.com/AmazonFresh

Instacart
Instacart.com

Shipt
Shipt.com

Paper Planners

Emily Ley Simplified Planner
EmilyLey.com/collections/simplified-planner

Erin Condren Life Planner
ErinCondren.com

Full Focus Planner
FullFocusPlanner.com

Happiness Planner
TheHappinessPlanner.com

Living Well Planner
LivingWellPlanner.com

Passion Planner
PassionPlanner.com

Productivity Printables

David Seah
DavidSeah.com/productivity-tools

Mom Agenda
MomAgenda.com/printable

Productive Flourishing
ProductiveFlourishing.com/free-planners

Sarah Titus
SarahTitus.com/category/printables-calendars

Smartsheet
Smartsheet.com/free-time-management-templates

Support Groups
Meetup
Meetup.com/topics/productivity

Productivity Boosters for Female Entrepreneurs
Facebook.com/groups/productivityboostersfor
femaleentrepreneurs

Websites
Brian Tracy
BrianTracy.com

I'm an Organization Junkie
OrgJunkie.com

Julie Morgenstern
JulieMorgenstern.com

Productive Flourishing
ProductiveFlourishing.com

Productivityist
Productivityist.com

Time Management Ninja
TimeManagementNinja.com

References

Chapter 2

Hindy, Joseph. "When You Stop Checking Facebook Constantly, These 10 Things Will Happen." http://www.lifehack.org/articles /communication/when-you-stop-checking-facebook-constantly -these-10-things-will-happen.html. Accessed March 13, 2019.

"The History and Evolution of SMART Goals." http://www .achieveit.com/resources/blog/the-history-and-evolution -of-smart-goals. Accessed March 13, 2019.

"How Many Times Are People Interrupted by Push Notifications?" http://www.askwonder.com/q/how-many -times-are-people-interrupted-by-push-notifications -58efcbf59682ca280093ebd9. Accessed March 13, 2019.

Moran, Brian P. *The 12 Week Year: Get More Done in 12 Weeks Than Others Do in 12 Months.* New York: Wiley, 2013.

Nield, David. "How to Find Out Which Apps and Websites You're Most Addicted To." http://www.gizmodo.com/how-to -find-out-which-apps-and-websites-youre-most-addi-1822667517. Accessed March 13, 2019.

Panganiban, Kix. "Quitting Facebook Made Me a Happier, More Productive Individual." http://www.medium.com /@kixpanganiban/quitting-facebook-made-me-a-happier -more-productive-individual-f8ee6016f7b1. Accessed March 13, 2019.

Veldhuijzen van Zanten, Boris. "This Hidden iOS Function Shows How Much Time You're Wasting on Which Apps." http://www .thenextweb.com/insider/2017/08/25/hidden-ios-function-how -much-time-wasting-apps. Accessed March 13, 2019.

Chapter 3

Ferriss, Timothy. *The 4-Hour Workweek: Escape 9–5, Live Anywhere, and Join the New Rich*. New York: Harmony, 2009.

Stuart, Annie. "Divide and Conquer Household Chores." http://www.webmd.com/parenting/features/chores-for-children. Accessed March 13, 2019.

Chapter 4

Aguirre, Sarah. "Conquering Clutter with the 4-Container Method." http://www.thespruce.com/conquering-clutter-the-4-container-method-1900130. Accessed March 15, 2019.

Kondo, Marie. "The KonMari Method." http://www.konmari.com/pages/about. Accessed March 15, 2019.

Walsh, Peter. "Peter Walsh's Organizing Ideas for Every Room in Your Home." http://www.oprah.com/home/organizing-tips-from-peter-walsh-declutter-your-home/all. Accessed March 14, 2019.

Chapter 5

"The Big Idea: Meetings, the Ultimate Time-suck, and How to Fix Them." TED Blog. April 04, 2018. Accessed March 20, 2019. https://blog.ted.com/meetings-the-ultimate-time-suck-and-what-to-do-about-them/.

"8 Tips for Conducting a Great Virtual Meeting." Journal of Accountancy. June 25, 2018. Accessed March 20, 2019. https://www.journalofaccountancy.com/newsletters/2018/jun/great-virtual-meeting.html.

"Help Me Run This Contentious Meeting!" Help Me Run This Contentious Meeting! - Meetings Business Conflict. https://ask metafilter.com/266379/Help-me-run-this-contentious-meeting. Accessed May 20, 2019.

"How Long Should a Meeting Be?" http://www.meetingking.com/how-long-should-a-meeting-be/. Accessed March 15, 2019.

Nelson, Lisa. "A Simple Facilitation Technique: The Parking Lot." http://www.seeincolors.com/a-simple-facilitation-technique-the-parking-lot. Accessed March 15, 2019.

Rolston, Matthew. "How to Look Good on a Webcam." https://www.youtube.com/watch?v=FMex-9FyljU. Accessed March 16, 2019.

Chapter 6

Cirillo, Francesco. "The Pomodoro Technique: Do More and Have Fun with Time Management." http://www.francescocirillo.com/pages/pomodoro-technique. Accessed March 16, 2019.

Mediakix. "How Much Time Do We Spend on Social Media?" http://www.mediakix.com/2016/12/how-much-time-is-spent-on-social-media-lifetime/#gs.qzkM2g1v. Accessed March 16, 2019.

Newport, Cal. "Have We Lost Our Tolerance for a Little Boredom?" http://www.calnewport.com/blog/2009/02/04/have-we-lost-our-tolerance-for-a-little-boredom. Accessed March 16, 2019.

Park, Jooyoung, Fang-Chi Lu, and William H. Hedgcock. "Relative Effects of Forward and Backward Planning on Goal Pursuit." http://www.journals.sagepub.com/doi/10.1177/0956797617715510. Accessed March 16, 2019.

Conclusion

Bilbray, Sandra. "The Happy Formula for Successful Kids." Live Happy Magazine. http://www.livehappy.com/relationships /parenting/happy-formula-successful-kids. Accessed March 16, 2019.

LaPorte, Danielle. "A Celebration of The Stop Doing List." https:// www.daniellelaporte.com/read/seth-godin-stop-doing-list. Accessed March 16, 2019.

Meinecke, Christine. "Self-Care in a Toxic World." Psychology Today. http://www.psychologytoday.com/us/blog/everybody-marries -the-wrong-person/201006/self-care-in-toxic-world. Accessed March 16, 2019.

Schwartz, Tony. "The Rhythm of Great Performance." The Energy Project. http://www.theenergyproject.com/the-rhythm -of-great-performance. Accessed March 16, 2019.

Thomas, Liji. "Circadian Rhythm Length Variations – Early Birds and Night Owls." New Medical Life Sciences. http://www .news-medical.net/health/Circadian-rhythm-length-variations -early-birds-and-night-owls.aspx. Accessed March 16, 2019.

Index

Acknowledgments

It's funny—in the back of my mind I had always dreamed of writing a book, but when the idea for this one was pitched to me, I initially said no. I didn't actually think I had an entire book inside of me. So thank you to the Callisto Media team for pushing me outside of my comfort zone and giving me the opportunity to write this book. Your persistence, patience, kindness, and wisdom throughout the entire process has been nothing short of stellar. I couldn't have asked for a better first publishing experience.

Little did I know how intense the writing process would be while running a business and managing my day-to-day life. I would not have been able to do it without the unconditional love and support of my husband and best friend, Jeff. Once again you have given me an opportunity to explore and expand my career beyond my wildest dreams, and I am eternally grateful for it. Thank you for believing in me and being my partner on this incredible journey together.

The whole reason my work-at-home journey began is because my daughter, Hadley, came into the world and I couldn't imagine leaving her in the care of someone else. Thank you for motivating me to take a leap of faith into the world of entrepreneurship; I've never been happier in my career or my life, and I owe a great deal of that to you.

I am so fortunate to have parents who taught me the value of hard work, being gracious, and acting with integrity. I appreciate everything you have done for me; without your guidance, I wouldn't be the person I am today.

They say if you have one true friend in your entire lifetime that you've been blessed. Well, I must have been extra nice in my past life because I am blessed with some of the best girlfriends in the world, who continually cheer me on and lift me up. Thank you for your unwavering encouragement and support.

Last, but not least, thank you to all my readers over at The Work at Home Woman—your recognition means the world to me.

About the Author

HOLLY REISEM HANNA is the publisher and creator of the award-winning website The Work at Home Woman, which helps individuals find remote careers and businesses that feed their souls. Holly is frequently quoted and interviewed in top media outlets like CNN, MSN Money, Huffington Post, and *Woman's Day* magazine. The Work at Home Woman was also recognized by Forbes as one of the "Top 100 Websites for Women." Holly resides in Austin, Texas, with her husband and daughter and enjoys reading, traveling, and yoga.

You can find out more by visiting her website at TheWorkAtHomeWoman.com.

Connect with Holly:
Facebook.com/TheWorkatHomeWoman
Instagram.com/thewahwoman
Twitter.com/Holly_Hanna

CPSIA information can be obtained
at www.ICGtesting.com
Printed in the USA
JSHW050751060421
13250JS00001B/2